W9-DCL-277

WITHDRAWN

English as a Second Language

Phase Three: Let's Write

English as a
Second Language

Phase Three:
Let's Write

William Samelson

San Antonio College

RESTON PUBLISHING COMPANY, INC., Reston, Virginia
A Prentice-Hall Company

Library of Congress Cataloging in Publication Data

Samelson, William, 1928-
    English as a second language, phase III.

    Includes index.
    1.   English language—Text-books for foreigners.
2.   English language—Composition and exercises.
I.   Title.
PE1128.S2174   428'.2'4   75-35712
ISBN 0-87909-263-7
ISBN 0-87909-262-9 pbk.

© 1976 by

RESTON PUBLISHING COMPANY, INC.

A Prentice-Hall Company
Reston, Virginia

10   9   8   7   6   5   4   3   2   1

Printed in the United States of America

For *Rosi*

Preface

ENGLISH AS A SECOND LANGUAGE, PHASE THREE: LET'S WRITE, is to be used as a text for a basic course in writing and composition for students of English as a second language. It is a pre-college text of English composition. The book is intended for a one-semester course though it can be used for intensive study courses also. This book aims at developing the student's vacabulary for better comprehension. It has been designed to offer the maximum limits of writing for the basic course.

It is a well-known fact that one does not write as one speaks, though both reading and writing are communication. Thus far, the student may have learned two types of vocabulary: 1. a *speaking* vocabulary (the most limited of the vocabularies), consisting of words used in conversation; 2. a *reading* vocabulary (larger than either the *speaking* or *writing* vocabularies), containing words that can be understood on sight even though one may not be able to use them in speech or writing. LET'S WRITE offers the student a third type of vocabulary: the *writing* vocabulary. This vocabulary is more extensive than that used in conversation. The present text reinforces structures learned through oral and reading comprehension while it introduces the student to the skill of writing.

Writing will be defined here as "the ability to use the language and its graphic representations in ordinary writing situations. More specifically, . . . writing a foreign language (is) the ability to use the structures, the lexical items, and their conventional representations, in ordinary matter-of-fact writing."*

Our aim is to provide the student with the ability to write independently and competently. To achieve the above objectives we undertake the following:

I.   To provide models of various types of composition (from simple one-paragraph types to the more complicated term paper), which the student will copy and ultimately learn to write independently.

II. To comment briefly on each MODEL COMPOSITION discussing distinguishing characteristics of style and organization. This will aid the students in their own writing and increase their comprehension of written material.

III. To suggest writing topics of broad and varying difficulty. This will allow the individual student to develop a writing skill reflecting his/her unique personality, background and attitude.

IV. To further enlarge the student's active vocabulary by providing alternate meanings for selected phrases and words. These are defined in the sense of the context of the MODEL COMPOSITION. Such contextual presentation reinforces the learning process, increasing the rate of retention and motivation.

To achieve the above objectives, each chapter (except CHAPTER ONE, THE WORD) comprises ten sections. Each section fulfills a unique function within the overall aim of this text.

I. MODEL COMPOSITION

The initial part of the chapter serves as an example of correct writing. Students will be expected to read the MODEL COMPOSITION with total comprehension if they are to write with reasonable skill at some future time. To achieve this goal, students will move forward cautiously through many "steps" under the guidance of their teacher. The suggested learning activities for this section are: 1. copying words or phrases; 2. copying sentences or paragraphs; and 3. writing from dictation. Exercises 2., and 3., are to be partially conducted in class under teacher's supervision.

II. WORDS IN CONTEXT

The vocabulary section comprises exercises in which the student must make considered lexical choices. Words are listed that are to be used to fill blanks in sentences. Where possible, an alternate word (*synonym*), or a phrase

---

*Robert Lado, *Language Testing*, McGraw-Hill, 1964, pp. 248-9.

that explains the meaning, may be used to fill a particular slot. The finished sentences are further altered by *substitution, replacement* or *transformation.*

III. STRUCTURES

Key words and phrases are expanded into complete sentences. This section also deals with groups of adjective-plus-preposition, verb-plus-preposition and noun-plus-preposition pairings that allow the student to generate new sentences.

IV. GRAMMAR and SYNTAX

Brief comments on the writing patterns and grammatical items contained in the MODEL COMPOSITION are made here. Further samples of writing are presented. These can be transformed by the student to express varying ideas, thus forcing production and encouraging the use of alternate vocabulary without altering syntactic structure. The student may supply all of the words on his vocabulary list that do not result in semantic absurdity.

V. IDEA RECOGNITION

Consideration is given here to the observation of logical syntactic and semantic relations within grammatically patterned sentences. The student is encouraged to develop new PATTERNS OF THOUGHT following the "kernal idea" extracted from the MODEL COMPOSITION. This practice will extend the student's sense of productivity, or creativity.

VI. VOCABULARY ENRICHMENT

To write effectively, the student learns new words. To retain these words, the student uses them repeatedly. In addition to providing the student with the useful vocabulary, all exercises within this text are organized in a manner to stimulate the student to review and reuse the expressions already learned.

This section includes some helpful techniques for vocabulary expansion. One of the exercises used is *paraphrasing* the MODEL COMPOSITION. The student completes sentences by furnishing synonyms or equivalents of a given term, thereby becoming aware that there are frequently alternate ways of expressing roughly the same idea in English.

Another helpful practice is the presentation of *lexical units*, i.e. words that may express related meanings through different structure.

> *Example:* His *name* is Mark Anthony.
> They *call* him Mark Anthony.

Recognition of *related* words in context or in isolation may prove useful in building an active writing vocabulary. Related forms of *NOUNS, ADJEC-TIVES* and *VERBS* are requested here.

Example request for related *noun*:	Cue:	*beautiful*
	Response:	*beauty*
Example request for related *adjective*:	Cue:	*study*
	Response:	*studious*
Example request for related *verb*;	Cue:	*runner*
	Response:	*run*

VII. STEPS TO WRITING

At this point, the student will learn to rephrase excerpted model sentences by the *addition* or *deletion* of words and the revision of sentences. Small grammatical changes may also be necessitated in the process. Thus, if a model sentence reads, "He studies at the university" the assignment may call for changing "he" to "we." This change will require a substitution of "study" for "studies."

A variety of assignments related to those described above are used to force semi-independent production. This should ultimately lead to free writing.

VIII. COMPREHENSION

The comprehension exercises comprise a sequence of procedural steps. Some call for the completion of a statement by choosing phrases from the MODEL COMPOSITION. The student then adds sentences related in context. Further, the student answers questions requiring a clear understanding of *ideas* contained in the MODEL COMPOSITION. These are exercises that do not require either the production of sentences or the composition of statements.

IX. COMMENTARY ON MODEL

The student is given key words or sentences from the MODEL COMPOSI-TION. He is to use them in his own composition on a topic related to that of the MODEL. Although the student may express agreement with the MODEL, he is encouraged to digress or disagree with the views of the model topic. This section constitutes partially guided writing; students are free to intro-duce an element of originality although they use known vocabulary and structures. As the students approach the final stages of the chapter, they should have enough "control of" the language to be able to manipulate what they have learned to express their own ideas and opinions.

X. COMPOSITION

At this point, the students are ready to be assigned a topic on which they will write a short composition. The extent of FREE COMPOSITION is determined by the students' qualifications. The students may title the resulting composition with an appropriate heading.

*　　　*　　　*

The "Let's" books have been prepared as a series; *Phase One: Let's Converse*; *Phase Two: Let's Read*; *Phase Three: Let's Write*. It is not necessary, however, to establish any one book as a prerequisite for the other. Each of the three books is independent of the others, and each may be used, according to the interests and needs of the students without reference to the other two books.

The "Let's" books are essentially student-oriented. However, the instructor must determine the most suitable way of utilizing the material provided here to the particular needs of the students. It is to be understood that the exercises presented in each chapter are to serve as points of departure for whatever needs arise. This can lead to a discussion of grammatical or morphological principles. It may also necessitate differentiation between formal and idiomatic terminology.

How much time is assigned to each exercise or chapter will depend on student needs and the nature of programs for which the text will be used. It is important, however, to complete each exercise as it is undertaken for the sake of total comprehension on the part of the student. The flexibility of the present material is one of the advantages of this text. It is easily adaptable to a variety of needs. But it should be understood that it is more advantageous to deal with a portion of the text exhaustively rather than with the entire text cursorily.

The handiest books to consult when writing are a good dictionary, a thesaurus and a reference grammar. Finally, we should remember that there is ONLY ONE WAY TO LEARN TO WRITE: THAT IS TO WRITE.

Acknowledgements

With this, the last of the "LET'S" ESL series, we have come to the completion of the trilogy (LET'S CONVERSE, LET'S READ, LET'S WRITE). While in the making, the project has taken us through three years of experimentation, writing, and revision. As promising as it is to begin work on a project that aspires to lighten the burdens of those in need of it, the more so gratifying it is to see it completed.

The most profound acknowledgements seem quite inadequate when one wishes to express gratitude for aid received. My appreciations go to Isabel Y. Vera Cruz for her helpful suggestions; to all my colleagues who tried the typescript experimentally in their classes during the 1974-75 school year and offered valuable suggestions and criticism; to my secretarial staff under the direction of Lucinda Cabasos for their help in typing the manuscript. Due recognition must be given Jaime Sustaita and Adan Reyna for their fine drawings; to my twelve year old son Henry for his drawing of the poem "Live for Death."

I wish to express my thanks to the executive branch of the Reston Publishing Co., Inc. for their trust in my ability as teacher and writer and to the production staff for their patient and able guidance through a labirynth of production pitfalls. The success of the "Let's" ESL series will be largely due to their combined efforts. I accept full responsibility for any shortcomings.

Finally, no acknowledgements would be complete without recognizing the efforts of my wife Rosita who so ably "filled in" with our four children, allowing me the freedom to pursue my work.

Contents

Chapter One

The Word

Words to Remember:

recognition – discrimination –

spelling – area of meaning –

root – stem – base – prefix –

suffix – word in context –

structure – composition – word

formation – change the meaning –

change part of speech

I. *Recognition and Discrimination*

In the beginning was the Word.
John 1:1

A. Composition

1. The desire to write goes one step beyond that of merely wishing to communicate: it allows us to share our knowledge, ideas, and feelings with the rest of the world. Writing also gives us the opportunity of becoming what we are, or may be.

2. In learning to write we must develop good habits as in learning to speak and to read. These habits can be formed only through practice. Observing the writings of others is only half the work; creating our own compositions is an essential activity in learning to write.

3. Let's not think that mastering a language simply means learning its vocabulary. Initially we learn to *recognize* certain basic often-used words. After that comes the time to expand our vocabulary. Words should never be studied in isolation. They are learned in relation to other words. Only then can we give full significance to a word.

4. The cosmopolitan nature of the English language is both an advantage and a disadvantage. Its advantage is that it has taken words from many sources, each with a precise definition. Its disadvantage lies in the fact that these words are often very nearly alike in definition. A writer not intimately familiar with their exact meanings will use them contrary to their correct usage.

5. It is important to use the right word in a given place. The correct definition of a term must be learned. Poor spelling is frequently the cause for misuse of words. Oftentimes, unable to spell the needed word correctly, we will use a poor compromise or an altogether wrong expression.

Examples of some commonly misspelled words are as follows:

Altogether means "thoroughly or completely."
All together means "everything or everybody collected."
 I'm not **altogether** sure I remember.
 They are **all together** at my home.
Already means "by the time" or "previously."
All ready means "completely ready" or "everything or everybody is ready."
 The sightseeing tour had **already** begun.
 The tourists were not **all ready** to travel.
Past refers to previous time or "farther than" or "beyond."
Passed is a form of the verb "pass," "successfully completed."
 It was **past** midnight when they called.
 They told me I **passed** my chemistry exam.

To indicates direction or is a marker of the infinitive verb.
Two is the number 2.
Too means that there is "more than enough" or "also."
> It took us **two** hours **to** drive from here **to** Jane's house.
> Her sister was there **too**. She told us that we stayed away **too** long.

Quite means "very" or "very much."
Quiet means "peaceful" or "not noisy."
> Misspelled words are **quite** frequently used.
> We can think much better when it's **quiet**.

Stationary means that something is "unchanging" or "fixed."
Stationery refers to "paper and envelopes used for letter writing."
> An acrobat seldom remains **stationary**.
> Each month I buy a box of **stationery**.

B. Composition by Degrees

1. a. Copy the title of the Composition I.A.
   _____

   b. Copy the sentence that tells what was "in the beginning."
   _____

2. a. Copy the sentence that tells us what we must "develop."
   _____

   b. Copy the sentence that tells how "habits can be formed."
   _____

   c. Copy the sentence that tells us what is an "essential activity."
   _____

3. a. Copy the sentence that tells us what we "initially" learn.
   _____

   b. Copy the sentence that tells how "words should not be studied."
   _____

4. a. Copy the phrase that tells of the "nature" of the English language.
   _____

   b. Copy the sentence that tells what *kind* of words English has borrowed.
   _____

   c. Copy the phrase that tells of the "disadvantage" of the English language.
   _____

5. Copy the sentence that tells what is "important."
   _____

4*The Word*

C. Vocabulary Enrichment

Identify the following words in the composition and copy them below as instructed in the first paragraph.

1. Copy all nouns.

_____

2. Copy all verbs.

_____

3. Copy words ending with *-ing*.

_____

4. Copy words ending with *-ed*.

_____

5. Copy words composed of more than one syllable.

_____

D. Lexical Units

Select the word or phrase from the following list that best completes each of the sentences below.

Example: He's not *completely* sure of it.
He's not *altogether* sure of it.

past	already	to
two	too	all together
quiet	quite	stationary
all ready	stationery	passed
altogether		

1. All the words are **collected** on this page. The words are _____ _____ on this page.
2. We have learned many words **previously**. We know many words ____ .
3. This composition is **completely** ready. It is ____ _____ .
4. He was there **after** midnight. It was _____ midnight.
5. She **successfully completed** her course. She _____ the final exam.
6. I've had **more than enough** to drink. I've drunk _____ much.
7. My friend **also** has a headache. He feels sick _____ .
8. It was a very **nice** party. It was _____ a party.

9. The neighbors asked us **not** to be **noisy**. They told us to be _____ .

10. We moved around a lot. Nobody stayed **fixed**. It is difficult to be _____ at a party.

11. Mother sent me some **letter writing** materials. I like my _____ very much.

E.   Related Words

Use the **related** words to rewrite the following sentences without changing their meaning. Change the underlined word(s). Make further changes if necessary.

       Example: Paul **uses** a poor compromise.
       Paul **is using** a poor compromise.

to communicate (v.)	to learn (v.)	to wish (v.)
communicating (n.)	learning (n.)	a wish (n.)
communication (n.)		wishing (n.)

to create (v.)	to expand (v.)	to develop (v.)
creating (n.)	expanding (n.)	developing (n.)
creation (n.)	expansion (n.)	development [of] (n.)

intimate (adj.)
intimately (adv.)

1. **Communication** is great fun.

2. **To develop** good habits is important.

3. It is one step beyond that of **wishing** to communicate.

4. **To create** compositions is essential.

5. **Learning** a language is not simple.

6. **The expansion** of our vocabulary comes later.

7. A writer must be **intimately familiar** with words.

F.   Answer these questions in writing. You may consult Composition A.

1. a. What do we share in writing?
   b. With whom do we share?
   c. What does writing do for us?

2. a. What must we develop in learning to write?
   b. How can good habits be formed?
   c. What is an essential activity in learning to write?

3. a. What do we learn initially?
   b. How can we give full significance to a word?
4. a. What is the advantage of a cosmopolitan language?
   b. What is the disadvantage of a cosmopolitan language?
5. a. What is important to use?
   b. What must be learned?
   c. What is the cause for the misused words?
   d. Why do we use a poor compromise?

G.   Write sentences using the words below.

1. desire _____

2. communicate_____

3. develop _____

4. initially _____

5. definition _____

6. compromise _____

II.   Spelling

Polonius: *". . . What do you read, my Lord?"*
 Hamlet: *"Words, words, words."*
                              Hamlet, Act II, Scene 2

A.   Composition

In LET'S WRITE we face the task of transferring our *speaking* and *reading* vocabularies into a *writing* vocabulary. This transfer involves hard work. Our task is important, because we know that we may be judged by the manner in which we use our language. It tells about our character and the ability of our minds. If we are careless in expressing our thoughts, it may be assumed that we are likewise careless in our thinking. At this point, examples of a few commonly misused words (because of ignorance of their correct spelling) are in order.

Accept* means "to take what is offered."
Except (verb) means "to exclude."

---

*All vocabulary definitions are based on the authority of WEBSTER'S NEW WORLD DIC-
TIONARY of the American Language; Second College Edition; World Publishing Co., and
Prentice-Hall, Inc., 1970.

We **accept** your invitation for dinner.

People can't get along, present company **excepted**.

Adapt means "to adjust, or to make fit."

Adopt means "to select, take up or assume as one's own."

To survive, one must constantly **adapt**.

We have **adopted** a new book for the English course.

Affect (verb) means "to influence, have an effect, or produce a change."

Effect (verb) means "to produce by an action, process or agent."

The cold **affected** all of us adversely.

The cold **effected** a change on all of us.

Beside means "by or at the side of, alongside."

Besides means "in addition; as well."

The boy walked silently **beside** his uncle.

No one walked with the man **besides** the boy.

Emigrate means "to leave a country."

Immigrate means "to come into a country."

Many people **emigrated** from Europe.

They **immigrated** to the United States of America.

Some words are misused and interchanged incorrectly because they share something in common.

Legible is something "that can be read or deciphered."

Readable is something "interesting and easy to read."

His new theme is **legible**. It is **not readable**, and I find it very **dull**.

Notorious means "widely but unfavorably known."

Famous means "much talked about; being favorably known, or being a celebrity."

Capone was a **notorious** gang leader of the thirties.

Jonas Salk is a **famous** scientist and developer of an antipolio vaccine.

Well as an adverb means "in a pleasing or desirable manner."

Well as an adjective means "in good health."

Mrs. Yancey hasn't been **well** lately, but she always treats people **well**.

Students of English as a second language may find spelling in English difficult because it is not quite phonetic. *Phonetic* means that there is a close correspondence between sound and symbol. There are some very simple rules for spelling, however, samples of which are introduced below. (For a more thorough discussion of spelling rules consult a good reference grammar.)

1. **One-syllable words** ending in a consonant double that consonant when

adding a suffix beginning with a vowel, if the consonant is preceded by a **single** vowel.

plan—   She planned to go to the movies. She's a good planner.
drop—   He dropped the money into the tray. They're dropping him from the team.
quit—   I'm quitting work early tonight. I'm not a quitter.
fat—   The more you eat, the fatter you get.
bat—   He is the best batter of the year. What's your batting average?
hit—   The pitcher pitched a no-hitter. His hitting isn't as good as it used to be.
ship—   He made a fortune in shipping. They shipped him overseas.
big—   The trees grow bigger every day.

2. Words ending in a final **e** that is not pronounced (i.e., take, give, love, sincere, nature), drop the -e when adding a **suffix beginning** with a **vowel**.

Sincerity in loving is as natural as taking and giving.

3. Words ending in -ce and -ge generally **keep** the unpronounced -e **before** suffixes beginning with the vowels **a, o, u**.

notice—   It was noticeable from the beginning.
courage—   He was courageous.

[Words ending in a final unpronounced -e generally keep that letter when the added **suffix begins** with a consonant; i.e., **pale**—The paleness was evidence of her long illness.]

4. Probably the most familiar of all spelling rules is "put **i** before **e**, except after **c**."

achievement— It was a great achievement
niece—   when my niece received her
receive—   college diploma.

[Note: There are many exceptions to the above "**c**" rule; i.e., **neither**, leisure, seize, etc.]

5. Words ending in -y preceded by a consonant, change final -y to i before adding a suffix **beginning** with a **vowel (except i)** or a **consonant**.

happy—	The secretary was happ**ier**
marry—	when she marr**ied**
library—	the librar**ian**.

6. The general rule for **nouns** ending in -y preceded by a consonant, to which the plural -s is added is to change the -y to **i** and add -**es**.

city + -s—	He lived in many **cities**.
industry + -s—	The U.S. has varied indus**tries**.
theory + -s—	There are different scientific **theories**.

(Exceptions are one-syllable words; i.e., bay + -s—**bays** and day + -s—**days**)

7. Words ending in -**c** take on -**k** when adding a **suffix** that **begins** with a **vowel**.

| picnic— | When we were picnic**king**, it rained and thundered, |
| panic— | and everybody panic**ked**. |

B. Composition by Degrees

1. Copy the title of Composition II.A.

_____

2. Copy the sentence that tells about the task we face here.

_____

3. Copy the sentence that tells about the transfer of vocabularies.

_____

4. Copy the sentence that contains references to our "character."

_____

5. Copy the sentence that tells about being "careless."

_____

C. Vocabulary Enrichment

Identify the following words in the composition and copy them below as instructed.

1. Copy all words ending with -**ing**.

_____

2. Copy all words ending with -**ed**.

_____

3. Copy all **adjectives** and the nouns they modify.

_____

4. Copy all **adverbs**.

_____

5. Copy all **nouns**.

_____

D.   Lexical Units

Select the word from the following list that best completes each of the sentences below.

Example: He did not **take what was offered**.
He did not **accept** it.

legible	accept	excepted
emigrated	readable	famous
beside	immigrate	well (adv.)
affects	besides	well (adj.)
adapt	adopts	

1. Everyone gets along well, **excluding** those present. They get along, those present _____ .

2. They make things **fit** the situation. They _____ to the situation.

3. The teacher **selects** a new book. He _____ the book.

4. Learning has an **effect** on people. It _____ them.

5. The boy walks **alongside** his father. He walks_____ him.

6. There was no one there **with** the man. No one _____him was there.

7. They **left the country** to go to the U.S. They_____for the U.S.

8. **Coming into a country** is not easy. It is difficult to _____ .

9. We were soon **in good health**. We became _____ .

10. They were treated **in a pleasing manner**. They were treated _____ .

11. I was **not able to read** his handwriting. It was not_____ .

12. Before going to sleep, I read something **interesting**. The book I read was _____ .

13. Washington was a **celebrity**. He was _____ .

E.   Spelling Exercises

1. a. Practice your spelling by completing the following words:

Example: sad + **-er** = **sadder**

plan + **-ed** _____

drop + **-ed** _____

quit + **-ing** _____

fat + **-er** _____

bat + **-er** _____

hit + **-er** _____

ship + **-ing** _____

big + **-er** _____

mad + **-er** _____

care + **-ing** _____

put + **-ing** _____

red + **-est** _____

sin + **-ing** _____

2. a. Practice your spelling by completing the following words:
Example: complete + **-ing** = **completing**

sincere + **-ity** _____

love + **-ing** _____

take + **-ing** _____

give + **-ing** _____

desire + **-able** _____

measure + **-able** _____

manage + **-ing** _____

notice + **-ing** _____

b. Practice your spelling by completing the following words:
Example: notice + **-able** = **noticeable**

courage + **-ous** _____

manage + **-able** _____

place + **-able** _____

advantage + **-ous** _____

trace + **-able** _____

pleasure + **-able** _____

outrage + -ous   _____

3. In each of the following words, circle the letter(s) relating to the spelling rule "put **i** before **e**, except after **c**." Recopy the word. Use a dictionary to find the meaning of any new words.

achievement   _____   receipt   _____

niece   _____   ceiling   _____

receive   _____   piece   _____

deceive   _____   believe   _____

conceive   _____   brief   _____

4. a. Practice your spelling by completing the following words:
    Example: happy + -**est** = **happiest**

deny + -ing   _____   happy + -**er**   _____

deny + -**ed**   _____   library + -**an**   _____

marry + -ing   _____   study + -**ed**   _____

carry + -ing   _____   cry + -**ed**   _____

marry + -**ed**   _____   beauty + -**ful**   _____

carry + -**ed**   _____   supply + -**er**   _____

b. Practice your spelling by completing the following words:
    Example: ferry + -s = **ferries**

city + -s   _____   salary + -s   _____

industry + -s   _____   lady + -s   _____

theory + -s   _____   story + -s   _____

supply + -s   _____   depository + -s _____

mystery + -s   _____   berry + -s   _____

fantasy + -s   _____   cherry + -s   _____

III. *Word Formation*

A. Composition

1. Many people use the word **chauvinist** nowadays but not everyone knows that it comes to us from the French language. Words such as **cliché, felony, bagatelle** and **intrigue** come from France too. These are only a few of the many important English words borrowed from other languages.

2. From Italy we have acquired such often-used words as **balcony, ditto, bandit, gusto** and **contraband**. The word **mosquito** originated in Spain, as did **corral** and **tornado**. Germany gave us such words as **kindergarten, waltz** and **blitzkrieg**. The word **blitz** is frequently used to designate a quick play in football.

3. From the Hebrew we have acquired such commonly used words as **amen, Sabbath** and **jubilee**. And from Arabia we received words such as **alcohol, algebra, coffee, ginger** and **zenith**. The American Indian also gave us many words. Among others, we have the expressions **tomahawk, tobacco** and **skunk**. Even from faraway China words came to us for some of our common household products; **tea, chop suey** and **soy** among many others.

4. The English language builds its own vocabulary with roots from Latin and Greek. A root (**origin** or **base**) of a word is that part of the word that contains the **core** of its meaning. We can understand the full meaning of a word more clearly when we observe how it was formed.

5. Learning the most common roots increases our ability to analyze the meaning of many words. For instance, knowing that the word **annus** means "year" in Latin, we will recognize the meaning in such English words as **annual, anniversary, biennial** (happening every two years or lasting two years), and **perennial** (lasting or active throughout the whole year, or continuing for a long time).

A few common roots from Latin that we can readily recognize in English words are:

Root	*Area of Meaning*	*English Derivatives*
amare	love	enamor, amateur
aptare	fit	adapt, inept
capere	take, accept	capture, capacity
civis	citizen	civilian, civilization
fortis	strong, brave	fortify, fortitude
judicium	judgment	judicious, judiciary

magnus	great	magnify, magnificent
mors	death	mortal, immortal
nomen	name	nominee, misnomer
pax	peace	pacify, pacific
populus	people	population, popular
sentire	feel	sentiment, sensation
sequi	follow	sequence, consecutive
similis	like	similar, assimilate
venire	come	convene, circumvent
videre	see	visible, audiovisual
vivere	live	vivid, survive, revive

6. Many common English words come from the Greek language. Knowing, for example, that the root **aster** means "star" and that the root **nomos** means "law," "order" or "knowledge," we can put together the word **astronomy** (literally meaning **the law of the stars**). If we know that the word **logos** means "study of" or "science of," the word **astrology** will make logical sense as the "study of the stars." Some frequently occuring Greek roots are:

Root	*Area of Meaning*	*English Derivatives*
anthropos	man	anthropology, misanthropy
aster, astron	star	astronomy, astronaut
bios	life	biology, biography
chroma	color	monochrome, chromosome
demos	people	democracy, epidemic
geo	earth	geography, geology
ramma	letter, written	telegram, monogram
heteros	other, different	heterosexual, heterogeneous
homos	same	homosexual, homogenized
kosmos	order, the world	cosmic, cosmos, cosmonaut
logos	study of, science of	psychology, biology
mania	madness	mania, maniac
micros	small	microscope, microfilm
nomos	law, order	economy, astronomy
onoma	name	synonym, antonym
philos	loving	philosopher, philanthropy
pseudes	false	pseudointellectual, pseudonym
psyche	mind, life, soul	psychic, psychology
tele	distant	telephone, telepathy
theos	god	theology, atheist

7. Significant also in the formation of words is the use of many **prefixes**

and **suffixes**. A **prefix** is a syllable, a group of syllables or a word united with or fixed to the beginning of another word to **change its meaning** or create a **new word**.*

> For example: stem—normal
> with prefix—**ab**normal

8. A **suffix** performs a function somewhat similar to the prefix, but is attached to the end of the word. Some of the roots we have listed here also serve as prefixes and suffixes of English words. The most frequently used prefixes and suffixes come to us from Latin, Greek and Anglo-Saxon. A few examples of some commonly used **prefixes** and **suffixes** are listed below:

Latin Origin

Prefix	*Area of Meaning*	*Current Word*
ab-	away from	abnormal, absent
ante-	before, in front of	antecedent, anterior
anti-	against, opposite	antisocial, antiseptic
bene-	well	benefit, benevolent
con-	with	conversation, coeducation
com-	before m, p, b	
col-	before l	
cor-	before r	
co-	means joint(ly) with	
contra-	against, opposite	contradict, contrary
de-	from, down (negative)	devalue, degrade, de-emphasize
dis-	apart, away, not (negative)	dismiss, disorder
ex-, e-	out from, former	exit, ex-president
in-	into, not	innocent
im-	before m, p, b	impossible
il-	before l	illiterate
ir-	before r	irregular
mal-	ill, bad, badly, wrong	malevolent, malformed
mis-	wrong, wrongly, not	misunderstand, mistrust
post-	behind, after	postpone, posterity
pre-	before, earlier, in front of	precede, predict
re-	back, again	repeat, return
super-	over, above, extra	supersonic, superficial
syn-, sym-	together with	synchronize, sympathy

*WEBSTER'S NEW WORLD DICTIONARY

trans-	across, over, through, beyond	transatlantic, transport
uni-	one	uniform, unilateral, university

Greek Origin

Prefix	*Area of Meaning*	*Current Word*
ana-	again, up, against	anarchy, anachronism
arch-	chief, primitive, the earlier	architect, archaic
cat-	down, downward	catastrophe, catapult
dia-	through, between	dialogue, diagonal
eu-	good, happy, well	eulogy, euphony
hyper-	extreme, over, above	hypertense, hyperbole
hypo-	under, below	hypodermic, hypothesis
meta-	after, beyond	metabolism, metathesis
neo-	new	neologism, neophyte
para-	beside	parapsychology, paradox
peri-	around, about	perimeter, periscope
poly-	many	polygamy, polysyllabic
syn-	with, together	synchronize, synonym

Anglo-Saxon Origin

Prefix	*Area of Meaning*	*Current Word*
be-	throughout, over	besiege, besmudge
for-	against, not	forget, forbid
mis-	error, defeat, wrong	misbehave, misconduct
out-	beyond, completely	outdo, outside, outbreak
un-	not	undo, unimaginative
under-	beneath, less than	underrate, undermine, undernourish
with-	from, against	withdraw, withhold, withstand

9. Usually a suffix **changes** the word into another **part of speech**. For example:

stem—normal (adj.)
with suffix—normal**ly** (adv.)

or

stem—terror (n.)
with suffix—terror**ize** (v.)

a. **Nouns** are derived from **verbs** through the addition of suffixes -tion, -ion, -sion and -ation:

compile	—	compilation
examine	—	examination
denounce	—	denunciation, etc.

and the suffixes -al, -se, -ment, -iture and -ance:

govern	—	government
refuse	—	refusal
expend	—	expense
judge	—	judgment
furnish	—	furniture
sever	—	severance, etc.

b. **Nouns** are derived from **adjectives** through the suffixes -ness, -ity, -ce and -cy:

happy	—	happiness
romance	—	romantic
fragrant	—	fragrance

c. **Adjectives** are derived from **nouns** by adding the suffixes -ful, -less, -ious, -ous, -al, -ic, -ish, -an, -ary and -ed:

hope	—	hopeful
sorrow	—	sorrowful
pay	—	payless
end	—	endless
joy	—	joyous
Poland	—	Polish
America	—	American
imagination	—	imaginary
fever	—	feverish

d. **Adjectives** are derived from **verbs** by adding the suffixes -able, -ible and -ive:

manage	—	manageable
reverse	—	reversible
evade	—	evasive
repair	—	reparable

e. **Verbs** are derived from **adjectives** by adding the suffixes -**ize, -en** and -**fy**:

| thick | — | thicken |
| solid | — | solidify |

f. Finally, **adverbs** are derived from **adjectives** by adding the suffix -**ly**:

handy	—	handily
suitable	—	suitably
angry	—	angrily
false	—	falsely
able	—	ably
memorable	—	memorably

10. There are many suffixes, as well as roots and prefixes, in the English language. We have only enough space here to mention a few of those commonly used. As we progress, we will learn new formations of words. For now, however, let's remember to examine old and new words in the following manner:

a. What is the **area of meaning** of the **root**?

b. What is the **area of meaning** of the **prefix**?

c. What is the **area of meaning** of the **suffix**?

d. What is the **meaning** of the **word in context**?

e. Answer the above four questions correctly and you'll never have to look up the word again.

B. Composition by Degrees

1. a. Copy the title of Composition III.A.

_____

b. Copy the foreign words.

_____

c. Copy the name of the country from which these words come.

_____

2. a. Copy the words that came from Italy.

_____

   b. Copy the words that originated in Spain.

_____

   c. Copy the words that came from Germany.

_____

   d. Copy the word that is used to describe a quick play in football.

_____

3. Copy the countries mentioned in this paragraph.

_____

4. a. Copy the sentence that tells about **roots**.

_____

   b. Copy the phrase that tells why we can understand the "meaning of a word."

_____

5. a. Copy the phrase that tells what happens when you "learn the most common roots."

_____

   b. Copy the words that originate from the Latin words **annus**.

_____

   c. Copy the phrase that means **biennial**.

_____

   d. Copy the phrase that means **perennial**.

_____

C.   Word Root

1. In the chart below, some of the most common **roots** are listed alphabetically. The area of meaning of the root is given. In the space provided on the right, write examples of words that are formed from the root. Try to find new words in the dictionary that have also been formed from the root words.

a. **Latin origin**

Example: **aptare**—fit—adapt, inept

Word Root	Area of Meaning	Examples
amare	love	_____

capere	take, accept	_____
fortis	strong, brave	_____
mors	death	_____
pax	peace	_____
sequi	follow	_____
similis	like	_____
venire	come	_____
videre	see	_____
vivere	live	_____

b. **Greek origin**

Example: **logos**—study of—logical, astrology

Word Root	*Area of Meaning*	*Examples*
anthropos	man	_____
aster	star	_____
bios	life	_____
demos	people	_____
heteros	other, different	_____
kosmos	order, world	_____
nomos	law, order	_____
onoma	name	_____
philos	loving	_____
pseudes	false	_____
psyche	mind, soul	_____
theos	god	_____

2. In the chart below, some of the most common **prefixes** are listed alphabetically. The area of meaning of the prefix is given. In the space provided on the right, write examples of words that use the prefix. Try to find new words in the dictionary that also use the prefix.

a. **Latin origin**

Example: **ante**—before, in front—antecede, antecedent, antedate

Prefix	*Area of Meaning*	*Examples*
ab-	away from	_____
anti-	against, opposite	_____
bene-	well	_____
con-	with	_____
contra-	against, opposite	_____
de-	from, down (negative)	_____

dis-	apart, away, not (negative)	_____
in-	into, not	_____
mal-	ill, bad, badly	_____
post-	behind, after	_____
pre-	before, earlier, in front of	_____
re-	back, again	_____
super-	over, above, extra	_____
syn-, sym-	together with	_____
trans-	across, over, beyond	_____
uni-	one	_____

b. Greek origin

Example: **arch-** —chief, primitive, the earlier—archaic

Prefix	*Area of Meaning*	*Examples*
ana-	again, up against	_____
cat-	down, downward	_____
dia-	through, between	_____
eu-	good, happy, well	_____
hyper-	extreme, over, above	_____
hypo-	under, below	_____
meta-	after, beyond	_____
neo-	new	_____
para-	beside	_____
peri-	around, about	_____
poly-	many	_____
syn-	with, together	_____

c. Anglo-Saxon origin

Example: **a-** —at, in, on, to—ahead, afoot, asleep

Prefix	*Area of Meaning*	*Examples*
be-	throughout, over	_____
for-	against, not	_____
mis-	error, defeat, wrong	_____
out-	beyond, completely	_____
un-	not	_____
under-	beneath, less than	_____
with-	from, against	_____

3. In the chart below, some of the most common **suffixes** are listed alphabetically in groups of varied significance. The area of meaning of the suffix is given. In the space provided on the right, write examples of words that use the suffix. Try to find similar new words in the dictionary.

a. **Abstract Nouns**

Example: -**ment**—government

Suffix	*Area of Meaning*	*Examples*
-acy	All these suffixes	_____
-age	signify **state of**, **act**	_____
-ance, -ancy	**of**, **quality of**.	_____
-ence, -ency		_____
-ation, -tion		_____
-ion, -sion		_____
-dom		_____
-hood		_____
-ice		_____
-ism		_____
-ment		_____
-ness		_____
-ship		_____
-ty, -ity		_____

b. **Concrete Nouns**

Example: -**art**—braggart

Suffix	*Area of Meaning*	*Examples*
-an, -ant	All these suffixes	_____
-ent	signify **one who does**.	_____
-ard, -art		_____
-ary		_____
-ee, -eer, -ess		_____
-er, -ar,		_____
-ier, -or		_____
-ic, -ist		_____
-ite, -yte		_____

c. **Adjectives**

Example: -**al**—cerebral

Suffix	*Area of Meaning*	*Examples*
-ac, -al, -an	All these suffixes	_____

-ar, -ary	signify **resembling, full,**	_____
-ful	**of, belonging to.**	_____
-ic		_____
-ish		_____
-ive		_____
-ory		_____
-able	All these suffixes	_____
-ible	signify **capable,**	_____
-ile	**able to.**	_____

d. **Verbs**

Example: **-ate**—facilitate

Suffix	*Area of Meaning*	*Examples*
-ate	All these suffixes	_____
-en	signify **to make.**	_____
-fy		_____
-ize		_____
-ise		_____

D. Parts of Speech

1. a. Change **verbs** into **nouns.** Follow the examples. Consult your dictionary for new words.

Suffix   *Examples*

Suffix					
-al	refuse	→ refusal	survive	→	_____
	arrive	→ arrival	approve	→	_____
	propose	→ _____	dismiss	→	_____
-ance	annoy	→ annoyance	signify	→	_____
-ence	refer	→ reference	exist	→	_____
	transfer	→ _____	sever	→	_____
	defer	→ _____	accept	→	_____
	attend	→ _____	disturb	→	_____
-ation	compile	→ compilation	relate	→	_____
-tion	examine	→ examination	nominate	→	_____
	isolate	→ isolation	except	→	_____
	compose	→ composition	consult	→	_____
	recognize	→ _____	emigrate	→	_____
	denounce	→ _____	define	→	_____
	realize	→ _____	resign	→	_____
-er	manage	→ manager	teach	→	_____
-or	learn	→ learner	speak	→	_____

	write	→ _____	read	→ _____
	initiate	→ _____	govern	→ _____
	direct	→ _____	create	→ _____
	develop	→ _____	employ	→ _____
-ment	develop	→ development	judge	→ _____
	govern	→ government	invest	→ _____
	pay	→ _____	agree	→ _____
	argue	→ _____	punish	→ _____
-sion	decide	→ decision	expand	→ _____
	impress	→ impression	divide	→ _____
	express	→ _____	profess	→ _____
	progress	→ _____	collide	→ _____
-y	deliver	→ delivery	discover	→ _____
	inquire	→ inquiry	recover	→ _____
	arm	→ _____	flatter	→ _____

b. Change **nouns** into **verbs**. Follow the examples. Consult your dictionary for new words.

-ize	economy	→ economize	drama	→ _____
	terror	→ terrorize	author	→ _____
	critic	→ _____	familiar	→ _____
	organ	→ _____	final	→ _____

2. Change **adjectives** into **nouns**. Follow the examples. Consult your dictionary for new words.

-ce	romantic	→ romance	fragrant	→ _____
-cy	supreme	→ supremacy	constant	→ _____
	brilliant	→ _____	coherent	→ _____
-ity	agile	→ agility	artificial	→ _____
	able	→ _____	gullible	→ _____
	fragile	→ _____	charitable	→ _____
	fatal	→ _____	curious	→ _____
-ness	bashful	→ bashfulness	sleepy	→ _____
	happy	→ happiness	pleasant	→ _____
	kind	→ _____	useful	→ _____
	childish	→ _____	cheerful	→ _____

3. Change **nouns** into **adjectives**. Follow the examples. Consult your dictionary for new words.

-ful	hope	→ hopeful	taste	→ _____
	sorrow	→ _____	waste	→ _____

	fancy	→	fate	→
	pain	→	tact	→
-less	pay	→ payless	tact	→
	end	→ endless	pain	→
	power	→	hope	→
	regard	→	sense	→
-ous	joy	→ joyous	danger	→
	beauty	→ beauteous	glutton	→
	generosity	→	fame	→
	advantage	→	outrage	→
-ious	ambition	→ ambitious	atrocity	→
	victory	→	curiosity	→
	courtesy	→	labor	→
	luxury	→	mystery	→
-y	nerve	→ nervy	shadow	→
	dirt	→ dirty	wealth	→
	cloud	→	guilt	→
-al	nature	→ natural	mechanic	→
	economy	→	music	→
	exception	→	origin	→
-ish	fever	→ feverish	fiend	→
	Poland	→ Polish	self	→
	child	→	fool	→

4. Change **verbs** into **adjectives**. Follow the examples. Consult your dictionary for new words.

	repair	→ reparable	notice	→
-able	manage	→ manageable	pleasure	→
	place	→	support	→
	trace	→	achievement	→
-ible	reverse	→ reversible	divide	→
	convert	→	impress	→
	force	→	attract	→
-ive	evade	→ evasive	imagine	→
	persuade	→	impress	→
	destruct	→	select	→

5. Change **adjectives** into **adverbs**. Follow the examples. Consult your dictionary for new words.

	handy	→ handily	angry	→ angrily
-ly	suitable	→	false	→
	able	→	memorable	→

common   → _____   new   → _____

6. **Summary** of **parts of speech**. Fill in the missing form of the word. Follow the example on top of the table. Consult your dictionary only if you are not sure of the correct form of the word.

Noun	*Verb*	*Adjective*	*Adverb*
economy	economize	economical	economically
_____	dramatize	_____	_____
_____	_____	hopeful	_____
_____	_____	_____	memorably
reversal	_____	_____	_____
_____	evade	_____	_____
_____	_____	memorable	_____
_____	succeed	_____	_____
_____	_____	_____	satisfactorily
consideration	_____	_____	_____
_____	_____	separate	_____

7. **Analyzing Words.** If necessary, use your dictionary to analyze the words in bold print. Write your analysis on the lines provided.

a. **amare**

(1) What is an **amorous** person?

_____

_____

(3) How is the word **amateur** related to **amare**?

_____

_____

(2) What is meant by the word **enamor**?

_____

_____

(4) Is the word **amiable** related to **amare**?

_____

_____

b. **logos–bios**

(1) What do we mean by saying "He is logical?"

_____

_____

(2) What does **biology** literally mean?

_____

_____

(3) Combine another root with **logos** and explain the meaning.

_____

_____

(4) Combine another root with **bios** and explain the meaning.

_____

_____

c. **anthropos—logos**

(1) What is the literal meaning of **anthropology**?

_____

_____

(2) How is **misanthropy** related to the root anthropos?

_____

(3) What is a "**logical**" person?

_____

_____

(4) What is another word for **misanthropy**?

_____

d. **con-, co-**

(1) What is **coeducation**?

_____

_____

(2) What is the literal meaning of **conversation**?

_____

_____

(3) What does **coexist** mean?

_____

_____

(4) What does **contradict** mean?

_____

_____

e. **mal-**

(1) What is the meaning of the word "**malfunction**?"

_____

_____

(2) How is **malevolent** related to the prefix **mal-**?

_____

_____

(3) Which other word(s) will express **maltreat**?

_____

_____

(4) What is the relation of **mal-** to **mis-**?

_____

_____

f. **fortis**

(1) What does **fortify** mean?

_____

_____

(2) What does **fortitude** mean?

_____

_____

(3) Is **comfort** related to **fortis**?

_____

_____

(4) What is a **fort**?

_____

_____

PART ONE

Writing the Sentence

Chapter Two

The Simple Sentence

Words to Remember:

Use: **declarative** – *makes a statement*

       interrogative – *asks a question*

       affirmative
                vs. negative
       assertive

       imperative – *command or entreaty*

       exclamatory – *expresses strong feelings*

Structure: *Simple sentence—one subject/one predicate*

              period (.)—capitalization—

   question mark (?)—exclamation mark (!)

merchants ~ ... ...
merchandize ; ...

I. Model Composition

A. Advertising

1. Advertising is an American way of life. Americans like advertising. People depend on advertising in their daily lives. People are consumers. The advertisers are manufacturers. Some advertisers are salesmen. Their merchandise needs advertising. Every product is advertised. Merchants buy ads for their products. Good advertising means success. Bad advertising can mean failure.

2. There are many ways to advertise. "Ads" come in different forms. Newspapers carry advertisements. Products are announced on TV and radio. Such announcements are called "commercials." Commercial radio stations are popular. They have a wide audience. Billboards carry much advertising. Merchants buy advertising space. It's a big industry. Many agencies furnish a variety of services. The first American advertising agency was established in Philadelphia, Pa., in 1840. Many advertising agencies are active in the U.S. today. Other advertising media include magazines and journals. Short films are produced for advertising.

3. The language of advertising is simple. Most ads have a basic appeal to children. Advertising can be funny. It tells you to eat well. It also shows you how to diet. It is contradictory. Some examples of advertising are:

a.
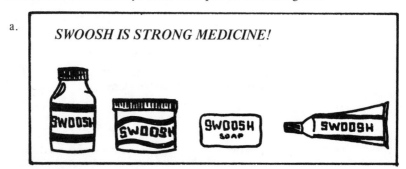
SWOOSH IS STRONG MEDICINE!

b.

NATURAL TASTE PASTRY IS GOOD!

c.

GOOD COFFEE IS IMPORTANT!

d.

HAVE YOU TRIED VIGOR CRACKERS?

4. Sometimes advertising is in the form of a dialogue. The following is an example: (Q. = question; A. = answer)

Q. Does your cereal taste good?

A. No, it doesn't.

Q. Have you tried another cereal?

A. No, I haven't.

Q. Haven't you heard of MATADOR CEREAL?

A. I've heard of it now and then.

Q. Why don't you try MATADOR CEREAL?

5. Advertising is not always truthful. A product is often misrepresented. The advertiser exaggerates the benefits of the merchandise he wants to sell. He misrepresents the truth. The consumer falls victim to advertising. Millions of people have bought advertised products. The people haven't always been satisfied. Most manufacturers guarantee their products. This is the way of free enterprise. Our business system is called the free enterprise.

B.   Composition by Degrees

1. a. Copy the title of the Model Composition.

   Advertising

   b. Copy the sentence that tells what "an American way of life" is.

   Advertising is an American way of life

   c. Copy the word that tells what Americans like.

   American like. advertising

   d. Copy the expression that tells what people "depend on."

   People depend on advertising in their daily lives

   e. Copy the words that tell who the consumers are and who the advertisers are.

   People are consumers, advertisers are manufacturer

   f. Copy the sentence that tells what is advertised.

   Every product was advertised

   g. Copy the sentence that tells what can "mean failure."

   _____

2. a. Copy the sentence that tells what the newspapers carry.

   _____

   b. Copy the sentence that contains the word "commercial."

   _____

   c. Copy the sentence that tells what the billboards carry.

   _____

   d. Copy the sentence that tells what the merchants buy.

   _____

   e. Copy the date that tells when the first advertising agency was established in America.

   _____

f. Copy the name of the city where the first agency was established in America.

_____

g. Copy the sentence that tells what radio stations are popular.

_____

3. a. Copy the word in sentence 1 that tells about the language of advertising.

_____

b. Copy the word in sentence 2 that is short for advertising.

_____

c. Copy the phrase that tells to whom ads appeal.

_____

d. Copy the name of the product advertised in ad "a."

_____

e. Copy the name of the product advertised in ad "b."

_____

f. Copy the name of the product advertised in ad "c."

_____

g. Copy the name of the product advertised in ad "d."

_____

h. Copy the sentences that make advertising funny.

_____

4. a. Copy the word that describes the advertising method in paragraph 4.

_____

b. Copy the name of the product advertised in paragraph 4.

_____

5. a. Copy the phrase that tells that advertising does not always "tell the truth."

_____

b. Copy the phrase(s) that tell(s) that a product is "shown to be different" from what it is.

_____

c. Copy the phrase that tells who buys advertised products.

_____

d. Copy the sentence that tells about free enterprise.

_____

II. *Words in Context*

A. From the list of words preceding each section, fill in each blank space provided in the text. You may use a selection more than once. Also, you may use more than one word in one blank space.

1. advertise(ment) need   depend(ent) failure
 advertising   consumers consume   ~~success~~

In America there is a _____ to _____. People _depend_ on _advertising_. Those who _advertise_ are manufacturers. Those who buy are _consumers_. People _____ many products. Good _advertising_ can mean _success_.

2. ~~different~~   advertise   advertisements ~~products~~
 "commercial" advertising ~~industry~~   variety
 ~~services~~   ~~agencies~~   produced   commercial
 media   ~~many~~

There are _many_ ways to _advertise_. Ads come in _different_ forms. Newspapers carry _advertisements_. Radio and TV announce _products_. Advertising on radio and TV is called "_commercial_". Merchants buy _advertising_ space. Advertising is a big _industry_. Many _agencies_ furnish a _variety_ of _services_. Other _advertising_ for _media_ are magazines and journals. Short films are _produced_ for _advertising_. _Commercial_ radio stations are popular.

3. language   appeal   advertising simple
 examples

The _language_ of advertising is _simple_. Most ads _appeal_ to children. There are many _examples_ of _advertising_.

4. tried   taste   dialogue try
 advertising another cereal

A _dialogue_ is sometimes _advertising_. Does your _cereal_ _taste_ good? Have you _tried_ _another_? Why don't you _try_ Matador _cereal_?

5. enterprise misrepresented truthful   exaggerates
 always   advertiser   victim   conceals
 product(s)   advertised   manufacturers consumer
 satisfied

Advertising is not _always_ _truthful_ . A _product_ is often _misrepresented_. The _advertisers_ _exaggerate_ about the merchandise. The _advertiser_ _misrepresent_ the truth. The _consumers_ falls _victim_ of advertising. Millions of people buy _____ products. The people are not always _____ . Most _____ stand behind their _____ . This is the way of free _____ .

B. Make the necessary change(s) when you substitute the new element into your sentence.

Example: Advertising is **an American** way of life. (a good way)
Advertising is **a good way** of life.

1. a. **Americans like** advertising. (Mary)
   b. People depend on **advertising**. (it)
   c. **People** are consumers. (they)
   d. **The advertisers** are manufacturers. (we)
   e. Their **merchandise** needs advertising. (products)
   f. **Every product** is advertised. (the merchandise)
   g. **Merchants** buy ads for their products. (advertisers)
   h. Advertising **means success**. (sells)

2. a. There are **many** ways to advertise. (few)
   b. Ads come in **different** forms. (varied)
   c. Products are **announced** on TV and radio. (advertised)
   d. Merchants **buy** advertising space. (need)
   e. Short films are **produced** for advertising. (made)
   f. **Commercial** radio stations are popular. (which advertise)

3. a. The language of advertising is **simple**. (easy to understand)
   b. Most ads **appeal** to children. (are appealing)
   c. Advertising can be **funny**. (comical)
   d. It tells you **how to eat well**. (about the good food)
   e. It also shows you how **to diet**. (not to overeat)
   f. The first agency was **established** in 1840. (founded)

4. a. Sometimes advertising takes the form of a **dialogue**. (conversation)
   b. Have you **tried** another cereal? (eaten)
   c. I've heard it **now and then**. (from time to time)

5. a. Advertising is **not always truthful**. (sometimes a lie)
   b. **A product is** often misrepresented. (products are)
   c. The advertiser exaggerates the benefits of the **merchandise** he wants to sell. (product)
   d. He **conceals** the truth. (hides)
   e. The **consumer falls** victim to advertising. (consumers)
   f. Millions of people **buy** advertised products. (purchase)

g. The people are not always **satisfied**. (pleased)
h. Most manufacturers stand behind their **products**. (merchandise)
i. This is the way free **enterprise** works. (commerce)

III.   *Structures (Key words [phrases] for composition)*

A.   Use the following key words [phrases] to form complete sentences. You may consult the MODEL COMPOSITION.

Example: advertising / is / way of life
Advertising is an American way of life.

1. a. America / likes_____
   b. people / depend / advertising _____
   c. people / consumers _____
   d. advertisers / manufacturers _____
   e. Some / advertisers / salesmen _____
   f. merchandise / needs / advertising _____
   g. product / is / advertised _____
   h. advertising / means / success _____
   i. bad / can / mean / failure _____
2. a. many / ways / advertise _____
   b. ads / come / different / forms _____
   c. newspapers / carry _____
   d. products / announced / TV and Radio _____
   e. are / called / commercials _____
   f. billboards / carry / advertising _____
   g. merchants / buy / space_____
   h. advertising / media / include / magazines / journals_____
   i. short films / are / produced / advertising _____
   j. commercial / stations / are _____
3. a. language / is / simple_____
   b. ads / appeal / children _____
   c. advertising / can be / funny _____
   d. it / tells / to eat / well _____
   e. shows / to / diet _____

    f. first / agency / established _____

4. a. does / cereal / taste _____

    b. have / tried / another _____

    c. haven't / heard / MATADOR _____

    d. why / don't / try / MATADOR _____

5. a. advertising / is not / truthful _____

    b. product / is / misrepresented _____

    c. advertiser / exaggerates / merchandise _____

    d. conceals / truth _____

    e. consumer / falls / victim / advertising _____

    f. people / buy / products _____

    g. are / not / satisfied _____

    h. manufacturers / stand / behind / products _____

    i. is / way / free / enterprise _____ _____

B. Supply the missing **prepositions** for each blank space. You may consult the MODEL COMPOSITION.

    Example: Advertising is an American way ___(of)___ life.

1. a. People depend _____ advertising _____ their daily lives.

    b. Merchants buy ads _____ their products.

2. a. Ads come _____ different forms.

    b. Products are announced _____ TV and radio.

    c. Many agencies furnish a variety _____ services.

    d. Short films are produced _____ advertising.

3. a. The language _____ advertising is simple.

    b. Most ads appeal _____ to children.

    c. These are examples _____ advertising.

    d. It tells you _____ eat well.

4. a. Haven't you heard _____ MATADOR cereal?

    b. I've heard _____ it now and then.

5. a. The advertiser exaggerates _____ the merchandise.

    b. The consumer falls victim _____ advertising.

    c. Millions _____ people buy advertised products.

    d. Most manufacturers stand _____ their products.

    e. This is the way _____ free enterprise.

IV. Grammar and Syntax [Points of Interest]

A. Correctness

    1. *Agreement*—Roots, prefixes and suffixes serve to form words. Sentences are formed from words. The **phrase** is the smallest unit from which a sentence is constructed. The smallest unit is called the **kernel**.

    Example: **The boy sings.**

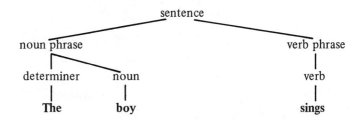

    The smallest *complete* sentence is called **simple**, or **declarative**.
    Example: **The man chased the dog.**

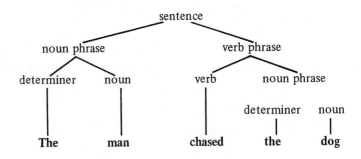

    A **simple** sentence has **one independent clause**. There are no dependent clauses attached. There may be modifying phrases. There is **one subject** and **one main verb**. The subject and the verb are in agreement.

Examples:

America	needs	advertising.
subject	verb	
The advertisers	are	manufacturers.
subject	verb	

There are four basic types of simple sentences in English. Their patterns are as follows:

SUBJECT	→ TENSE and BE	→ COMPLEMENT or	→	ADVERBIAL
(Noun	→ or VERBAL	→ DIRECT OBJECT	→	(optional)
Phrase)		(Noun Phrase)		

Examples of the four basic types of simple sentences are:

a. Type **be**	People	**are**	consumers	(usually).
	Merchants	**are**	advertisers	(always).
b. Type **verb intransitive**	Manufacturers	**stand**	behind their products	(often).
c. Type **verb transitive**	Americans	**like**	advertising	(every day).
	Merchants	**buy**	ads	(yearly).
d. Type **verb linking**	Advertisers	**seem**	honest	(usually).
	Merchants	**become**	advertisers	(usually).

2. *Transformations*—The above examples show simple sentence structure in English. These simple sentences can undergo transformations. Transformations change the structure of sentences. They delete, rearrange, add or substitute some of the items within the simple sentence.

    a. *Declarative*—A declarative sentence makes or denies a statement. Examples:

> *Everyone likes advertising.*
> *The advertisers are manufacturers.*
> *Merchants buy ads for their products.*

    b. *Interrogative*—The interrogative is the ordinary pattern for asking questions. Examples:

> *Does everyone like advertising?*
> *Are the advertisers manufacturers?*
> *Do merchants buy ads for their products?*
> *Going on a diet?*
> *Have you tried VIGOR crackers?*

c. *Affirmative (assertive)*—The affirmative is like the declarative. Its purpose is to express fact and opinion. The affirmative can be expressed in several ways. Examples:

> *What* an advertisement!
> *What* a good buy!
> *How* many ways to advertise!
> *How* I love it!

The **what** and **how** affirmatives express emotion. Both the **what** and the **how** of the affirmative are close to the meaning of the word **extraordinary**. Some examples of the above can be expressed in the following way:

> It is an **extraordinary** advertisement.
> It is an **extraordinary** buy.

d. *Negative*—The word *not* is the basic clause negator.

> Did you see the advertising?
> No, I *didn't* (did *not*) see it.
> I *don't* (do *not*) like cereal.
> Pastry *isn't* (is *not*) good.

The word *not* is not the only negator. A subject can also be a negator.

(1) *Not everybody* likes commercials.

(2) *Nobody* likes commercials.

The two sentences are different in meaning. The first one can mean almost everybody. The *no* in the second sentence expresses the meaning of *zero*. Some more examples are:

(1) Advertising *won't* (will *not*) get you anywhere.

(2) Advertising will get you *nowhere*.

(1) We *don't* (do *not*) have any money.

(2) We have *no* money.

(1) I *didn't* (did *not*) see anything.

(2) I saw *nothing.*

3. *The Tenses**–Differences in *time* are called *tenses.* Time is commonly referred to as *past, present* and *future.* The tenses are:

a. Present	→	I (do) need advertising.
		He (does need) needs advertising.
b. Past (simple)	→	I needed (I did need) advertising.
c. Future	→	I will (I'll) need advertising.
d. Present Perfect	→	I have (I've) needed advertising.
		He has needed advertising.
e. Past Perfect	→	I had needed advertising.
f. Future Perfect	→	I will (I'll) have needed advertising.

All of the transformations can be applied to the six tenses. Example:

(Present)
I need advertising.   → Do I need advertising? (Interrogative)
                          I don't need advertising. (Negative)

(Present Perfect)
I have needed advertising. → Have I needed advertising? (Interrogative)
                              I haven't needed advertising. (Negative)

[For other tenses follow the examples you've learned.]

B.   Completeness

The sentence must satisfy the following requirements:

1. It gives a sense of completeness.

2. It makes sense when you read it.

3. It has a subject (someone or something).

4. It has a verb (does something).

---

*Verb Tense is extensively discussed in Chapter Five. Here we will only discuss the basic concepts of six primary tenses in the *indicative.*

5. It begins with a capital letter.

6. It ends with a period or other terminal (end) punctuation mark.

Examples:

1. Merchants buy ads for their products.

2. Bad advertising can mean failure.

3. There are many ways to advertise.

4. Products are announced on TV and radio.

5. Swoosh is strong medicine!

6. Have you tried VIGOR crackers?

7. I haven't heard of it.

8. Does your cereal taste good?

C.   Punctuation

1. *The period* (.)—The period is an important mark of punctuation. It is used to end sentences or statements. Examples:

> The language of advertising is simple.
> Ads come in different forms.
> Most ads appeal to children.

Periods are used after independent clauses and dependent clauses. Examples:

> "Going on a diet?" "As soon as possible." (dependent)
> Everyone likes advertising. (independent) The sooner, the better. (dependent)

Periods are used with abbreviations. The period shows that a word has been shortened. Some examples are:

Rev.	=	Reverend
Dr.	=	doctor
Mr.	=	Mister
Ms.	=	married or unmarried woman
etc.	=	*et cetera* and so forth
e.g.	=	*exempli gratia*, for example
et al.	=	*et alii* and others
i.e.	=	that is

vs.	=	versus
Ph.D.	=	Doctor of Philosophy
Tex.	=	Texas
M.D.	=	Doctor of Medicine
a.m.	=	morning
p.m.	=	afternoon, evening
jr.	=	junior
sr.	=	senior
Inc.	=	Incorporated
Pa.	=	Pennsylvania

[NOTE: Never use the period to mark abbreviations when the period is not part of the official name. Some abbreviations have been discontinued.]

2. *Question mark* (?)—A question mark is used after a direct question. Examples:

> Have you tried VIGOR crackers?
> Does your cereal taste good?
> Haven't you heard of MATADOR cereal?

The most common direct question in English is the **WH** question. Examples:

> **Where** are you going?
> **How** are you?
> **What** have we here?
> **Why** aren't you ready?
> **When** will you come?

3. *Exclamation mark* (!)—In section A2(c) we used the exclamation mark as the end punctuation for the **what** and **how** affirmative sentence. The exclamation is used only after statements expressing **unusual emphasis**. Examples:

> Natural taste pastry is good!
> Good coffee is important!
> Swoosh is strong medicine!
> Do not conceal the truth!
> Think! Do it!
> You must not kill!

D. Capitalization

1. We capitalize the first letter of a word at the beginning of a sentence.

The advertisers are manufacturers.
There are many ways to advertise.

2. **A proper noun** (name of person, place, thing or animal) is capitalized. An **adjective** derived from that noun is also capitalized.

> There are many advertising firms in America (n.).
> The first American (adj.) advertising agency was established in 1840.
> Winter is very long in Alaska (n.).
> Alaskan (adj.) winter is long.
> Sam Houston was born in Texas (n.).
> Sam Houston was a Texan (adj.).

[NOTE: Proper nouns are days of the week, months, political parties, nationalities, societies, organizations, institutions, countries, cities, religions, corporations, geographic areas, states, etc.]

Examples:

> On Saturday he addressed the Democratic Party.
> Their first advertising appeared in May.
> The West is more populated than the East.
> Last July we climbed the Rocky Mountains.

E.   Exercises

1. *Subject-verb agreement*—Underline the correct verb form.

    a. Advertising (is/are) an American way of life.

    b. America (need/needs) advertising.

    c. People (is/are) consumers.

    d. The advertisers (is/are) manufacturers.

    e. Merchants (buy/buys) ads for their products.

    f. Advertising (mean/means) success.

    g. Ads (come/comes) in different ways.

    h. Newspapers (carries/carry) advertisements.

    i. Many agencies (furnishes/furnish) a variety of services.

2. *Transformations*—Transform the following sentences.

    a. Declarative to interrogative:

(1) Advertising is a way of life.

_____

(2) America likes advertising.

_____

(3) The advertisers are manufacturers.

_____

(4) Merchants buy ads for their products.

_____

(5) Their merchandise needs advertising.

_____

b. Affirmative to negative:

(1) That's a good buy!

_____

(2) This is the way to advertise!

_____

(3) I love it!

_____

(4) This is an extraordinary advertisement!

_____

(5) That's delicious coffee!

_____

3. *The Tenses*—Rewrite the following sentences using the tense given in parentheses.

a. There are many ways to advertise. (were)

_____

b. Ads come in different forms. (came)

_____

c. Products are announced on TV and radio. (have been)

_____

d. Commercial radio stations are popular. (will be)

_____

e. The language of advertising is simple. (has been)

_____

f. It tells you to eat well. (told)

_____

g. It also shows you how to diet. (showed)

---

h. The first agency was established in 1840. (had been)

---

i. Good coffee is important. (will be)

---

j. Advertising hasn't always been truthful. (isn't)

---

k. A product is often misinterpreted. (was)

---

l. The advertiser conceals the truth. (had concealed)

---

m. The consumer falls victim to advertising. (has fallen)

---

n. The people haven't always been satisfied. (aren't)

---

o. This is the way of free enterprise. (will be)

---

4. *Completeness*—Write a complete sentence for each of the following fragments. Refer to the MODEL COMPOSITION if necessary. All of the fragments can be found in paragraphs 1 and 2.

a. is an American way of life

---

b. depend on advertisement in their daily life

---

c. are manufacturers

---

d. product is advertised

---

e. buy ads for their products

---

f. bad advertising means failure

---

g. are many ways to advertise

---

h. carry advertisements

---

i. buy advertising space

_____

j. other advertising mediums magazines and journals

_____

5. *Punctuation*—Punctuate the following passage. Use only **periods** (.), **question marks** (?) and **exclamation marks** (!). Capitalize where you think it necessary. The number on the right indicates how many corrections are needed.

mr. Jones needed some advertising He was a manufacturer.	2
Mrs Jones worked at the methodist Hospital She was a nurse.	3
the M D's name was hendricks He was a specialist Mr. jones	7
bought two ads. he manufactured nuts, bolts, etc Business	2
wasn't good. mr and mrs. Jones hoped the advertising would	3
help their business	1
What do you like the man asked	3
I like to buy an ad Mr Jones replied	3
What size ad would you like	1
I prefer a small one Said mr. jones.	3
it was a hard day. Mr and Mrs. Jones were glad it was over	3
They had worked from 7 a m to 6 p m. They were tired	3

V. *Idea Recognition*

Copy from the MODEL COMPOSITION the sentences expressing:

A. an American way of life . . .

_____

B. why America likes advertising . . .

_____

C. who the manufacturers are . . .

_____

D. what good advertising means . . .

_____

E. what bad advertising means . . .

_____

F. in what forms ads come . . .

_____

G. what the radio and TV announcements are . . .

_____

H.   what kind of films for advertising are produced . . .

_____

I.   about the advertising language . . .

_____

J.   to whom advertising language appeals . . .

_____

K.   how advertising can be . . .

_____

L.   how advertising hasn't always been . . .

_____

M.   what the advertiser exaggerates about . . .

_____

N.   what the advertiser conceals . . .

_____

O.   the satisfaction of the people . . .

_____

VI.   *Vocabulary Enrichment*

A.   Paraphrasing

Paraphrasing involves rephrasing specific expressions or words without changing their meaning. Write the expressions found in the MODEL COMPOSITION that correspond to the paraphrases below.

Example: a way of life   **It is the way people live.**

1. people who buy things ___*is eversummer*___
2. people who tell about things ___*is advertisers*___
3. people who sell things ___*Seal man*___
4. good advertising ___*is sucess*___
5. bad advertising ___*is failure*___
6. announcements on radio ___*is "a comeraial"*___
7. people who sell advertising_____
8. doing the advertising _____
9. can be easily understood ___*is appeal to children.*___
10. don't tell the right thing _____

B. Lexical Units

Select the word (phrase) from the following list that best completes each of the sentences below. You may use a selection more than once.

Example:

They **exaggerate** about their product.
They **misrepresent** the truth about it.

tell	~~way of life~~	dependent	sell
advertising	commercial	widely	contradictory
basic	conversation		

1. America **likes** advertising. It is an American _way of life_ .
2. People **depend** on advertising. They are _dependent on advertising_.
3. The manufacturers **advertise**. They _tell_ about their product.
4. The salesmen **advertise**. They want to _contradictory_ merchandise.
5. Products are **announced** on radio and TV. This is called a _commercial_
6. Magazines carry **announcements**. They are a medium for _advertising_.
7. Commercial radio stations are **popular**. They are _widely_ listened to.
8. The language of advertising is **simple**. Its structure is _basic_ .
9. Advertising is sometimes **funny**. This happens when advertising becomes _conversation_ .
10. Some ads are presented as **dialogues**. People understand _it_ better than pictures.

C. Related Words

Use the **related words** to rewrite the following sentences without changing their meanings. Change the underlined word. Make further changes if necessary.

Example: to buy (v.)   buyer (n.)
          Merchants **buy** much advertising.
          Merchants are **buyers** of much advertising.

to advertise (v.)	to produce (v.)	to establish (v.)
advertising (n.)	products (n.)	establishment (n.)
advertisement (n.)	production (n.)	
to succeed (v.)	to consume (v.)	to fail (v.)
success (n.)	consumer (n.)	failure (n.)

to depend (v.)   to announce (v.)
 dependence (n.)   announcements (n.)
 dependent (adj.)

1. **Advertising** is a necessity. _____
2. Without ads they **fail**. _____
3. They **announce** products on TV. _____
4. They **depend** on advertising. _____
5. Advertising helps **succeed**. _____
6. What they **produce** is good. _____
7. The public **consumes** products. _____
8. There are old **established** firms. _____

VII. Steps in Writing

A. Add new words and revise the sentence to suit the changes indicated in parentheses.

Example: **America** likes advertising. (Americans)
          Americans **like** advertising.

1. **The consumer** needs advertising. (consumers)

   _____

2. **People** depend on advertisement. (He)

   _____

3. **They** are consumers. (She)

   _____

4. **Every** product is advertised. (some)

   _____

5. Merchants **buy** ads for their products. (need)

   _____

6. Ads **come in different forms**. (are differently formed)

   _____

7. **Newspapers** carry advertisements. (our newspaper)

   _____

8. **Many agencies** furnish a variety of services. (My agency)

   _____

9. **They have** a wide audience. (their audience is)

   _____

10. **Their language is simple.** (they speak simply)

_____

11. **Ads** have a basic appeal to children. (advertising)

_____

B.   Opposites

Use the **opposites** to rewrite the following sentences. Make the necessary changes to suit the new sentences.

> Example: likes—dislikes
>   America likes advertising.
>   America **dislikes** advertising.

sad	agreeable	complicated	few	tells the truth
limited	bad	unimportant	weak	never
satisfied				

1. The language is **simple.** _____

2. **Most** ads appeal to children. _____

3. Ads can be **funny.** _____

4. It is often **contradictory.** _____

5. They have a **wide** audience. _____

6. Natural taste pastry is **good.** _____

7. Swoosh is **strong** medicine! _____

8. Good coffee is **important!** _____

9. The advertiser **lies** about the product. _____

10. People are **always** satisfied. _____

11. Sometimes they are **dissatisfied.** _____

VIII.   Comprehension

A.   Complete the sentence and add as many related sentences as you can find in the MODEL COMPOSITION.

> Example: Advertising is an **American way of life.**
>   America likes advertising. People depend on advertising in their daily life.

1. Merchants buy ads _____

_____

2. Products are announced on TV _____

3. The first American advertising agency was established _____

4. Commercial radio stations are _____

5. The language of advertising is _____

B.   Reply with complete sentences.
       Example: Who advertises?
                  Merchants and salesmen advertise.

1. Why do people depend on advertising? _____

2. What happens with bad advertising? _____

3. Are there many ways to advertise? What are they? _____

4. How do we know that commercial radio stations are popular? _____

5. What is the language of advertising? _____

6. Why is some advertising funny? _____

7. What does ad "a" say about "Swoosh?" _____

8. What does ad "d" advertise? _____

9. Has advertising always been truthful? _____

10. What often happens to an advertised product? _____

11. What happens to the consumer when truth is misrepresented? _____

12. Have the people always been satisfied? _____

13. Do most manufacturers stand behind their products? _____

14. What is our business system called? _____

_____ _____

IX. *Commentary on Model*

A. 1. Describe ad "a."

2. Describe ad "d."

3. Discuss the importance of advertising.

4. Discuss why the language of advertising is simple.

5. Give an appropriate title to your composition.

B. 1. Discuss the points in the MODEL COMPOSITION that you like.

2. Discuss the points in the MODEL COMPOSITION with which you disagree.

3. Tell briefly what you think about advertising.

4. Give an appropriate heading to your composition.

X. *Composition*

A. Using the key words and phrases from the MODEL COMPOSITION, write your own composition on a related topic.

way of life	depend on advertisement	consumers
manufacturers	salesmen	success
products	bad advertising	commercials
failure	TV and radio	popular
advertising space	variety of services	established
simple language	contradictory	public falls victim
misrepresent	exaggerate	

B. 1. Rewrite section 1 of the MODEL COMPOSITION in the **I** person. Make all appropriate changes.

Example: Advertising is **my** way of life.

2. Rewrite section 4, changing singular forms to their plural forms (i.e. **product** to **products**, **advertiser** to **advertisers**, etc.). Make all appropriate changes.

C.   Describe briefly what you see in the picture below.

Chapter Three

The
Compound Sentence

Words to Remember:

compound = *two or more main*

(independent) clauses

Coordination—Coordinators

and, but, for, nor, or, so, yet

Parallelism—Faulty Parallelism

semicolon (;) comma (,)

hyphen (-)

I. *Model Composition*

"I think; therefore I am."
Descartes

A. Creative Thought

1. What is thought? The question is as old and puzzling as man himself. The other day I heard someone say, "This is food for thought." What did that mean? It was, perhaps, a way to encourage creative thought.

2. There are many ways in which our thinking is stimulated. To be productive individuals, we must think. When we study English, we think. We speak and create new thoughts. We write and think only in English. Thinking in one language, but learning another, makes it harder to progress creatively. When we study English, we must think in English.

3. Once I walked slowly and leisurely across a large meadow. There were many flowers and trees in bloom. The landscape looked peaceful and inviting. I was in a hurry, but not seeing anyone present, I remained for a while. Thoughts came to me readily, and I felt creative. There was silence around me, but there was a very special "buzzing" in my mind. That "buzzing" I called thought. Some people call it meditation.

4. The other day there were twenty-one children on the meadow. They were very noisy. One small boy was from Indiana; the others were Texans. I guessed that, because the Texans called the small boy "Hoosier." I listened to him, and he was glad. His father was an attorney-at-law in a small town. His grandfather took part in the Spanish-American War. The boy was proud of his heritage.

5. I wondered why the small boy confided in a stranger; I was a stranger to him. Now it was quiet on the meadow. There was no one present to disturb me. People are lonely, I thought. They need someone to talk to, yet they seldom listen. We must listen to children, so that we can understand them. We are called "thoughtful" when we are considerate and listen.

6. Not all thinking is creative. A painter creates his work in his thoughts, so does a writer, or a dancer. That is creative thought. But a person can simply think before he acts; that kind of thought is called "wisdom." When people think and listen, they commit fewer mistakes. Many misunderstandings are avoided this way. In a manner of speaking, this type of thought can be called creative too. Things that are not destructive may well be considered creative.

B. **Composition by Degrees**

1. a. Copy the title of the MODEL COMPOSITION. _____
_____

 b. Copy the sentence that tells what is "puzzling." _____
_____

 c. Copy the sentence that tells the meaning of "food for thought." __
_____

2. a. Copy the sentence that tells what individuals must do to be productive. _____
_____

 b. Copy the sentence that tells what makes it harder to "progress creatively." _____
_____

 c. Copy the sentence that tells what we must do when "we study English." _____
_____

3. a. Copy the sentence that tells where the narrator walked. _____
_____

 b. Copy the sentence that tells what looked "peaceful and inviting."
_____

 c. Copy the sentence that tells in what manner the narrator's thoughts came. _____
_____

 d. Copy the phrase that tells how the narrator felt. _____
_____

 e. Copy the phrase that tells what was on the narrator's mind. _____
_____

 f. Copy the phrase that tells what the narrator called the "buzzing."
_____

4. a. Copy the phrase that tells how many children were on the meadow.
_____

 b. Copy the phrase that describes how the children were. _____
_____

 c. Copy the phrase that describes the boy from Indiana. _____
_____

 d. Copy the sentence that tells the profession of the boy's father.
_____

5. a. Copy the phrase that tells what the narrator wondered. _____

b. Copy the sentence that tells how people are. _____

c. Copy the sentence that tells what people need. _____

d. Copy the sentence that tells what we must do with children. _____

e. Copy the phrase that tells what we are called when we listen. _____

6. a. Copy the sentence that tells how a painter creates his work. _____

b. Copy the sentence that tells what a person can do before acting.

c. Copy the sentence that tells what happens when we "think and listen." _____

d. Copy the phrase that tells what the things are called that are "not destructive." _____

II. Words in Context

A. From the list of words and phrases preceding each section, fill in each blank space provided in the text. You may use a selection more than once. Also, you may use more than one word in one blank space.

1. puzzling   other   perhaps   creative
   someone   thought   encourage

The question about_____ is as old and _____ as man himself. The _____ day I heard _____ say, "This is food for_____ ." It was, _____, a way to_____ _____ _____ .

2. thinking   think   create   productive
   learning   progress

Our _____ is stimulated in many ways. To be _____ individuals, we must _____ . When we study English, we _____ . We write and _____ only in English. _____ in one language, but _____ another, makes it harder to _____ creatively.

3. leisurely   peaceful   hurry   remained
   seeing   thought(s)   silence   "buzzing"

Slowly and _____ I walked across a large meadow. The landscape looked _____ and inviting. I was in a _____ , but not _____ anyone present, I remained for a while. _____ came to me. There was _____ , but there was a very special _____ in my mind. That _____ I called _____ .

4. twenty-one   listened   glad   noisy   boy
   attorney-at-law   proud   heritage   Spanish-American

There were _____ children on the meadow. They were _____ . One small _____ was from Indiana. I _____ to him, and he was _____ . His father was an _____ . His grandfather took part in the _____ War. The boy was _____ of his _____ .

5. quiet   considerate   disturb   lonely
   confided   seldom   "thoughtful"   stranger
   thought   listen   wondered

I _____ why the boy _____ in me. I was a _____ to him. Now it was _____ on the meadow. There was no one _____ to _____ us. People are _____ , I _____ . They _____ listen. We must _____ to children. We are_____ called_____ when we are _____ and_____ .

6. thought(s)   think   commit   misunderstandings
   creative   listen   acts   considered
   destructive thinking   creates

Not all _____ is _____ . The painter _____ his work in his _____ . A person can simply _____ before he _____ . When people _____ and_____ they _____ fewer mistakes. Many _____ are avoided this way. This type of _____ can be called_____ too. Things that are not _____ , may well be _____ _____ .

B.   Make any necessary change(s) when you substitute the new element into your sentence.

      Example: I think; therefore I **am.** (exist)
                  I think; therefore I **exist.**

1. a. What **is thought**? (thoughts) ⎯⎯⎯⎯⎯⎯⎯⎯⎯
_____

   b. The question is as old and puzzling as **man**. (ourselves) ⎯⎯⎯⎯
_____

   c. What did **that** mean? (it) ⎯⎯⎯⎯⎯⎯⎯⎯⎯⎯
_____

   d. It was **a way** to encourage thought. (meant) ⎯⎯⎯⎯⎯⎯
_____

2. a. Our **thinking is** stimulated. (thoughts) ⎯⎯⎯⎯⎯⎯⎯
_____

   b. To be **productive**, we think. (creative) ⎯⎯⎯⎯⎯⎯
_____

   c. **When we study** English, we think. (while studying) ⎯⎯⎯⎯
_____

   d. We speak and create new **thoughts**. (ideas) ⎯⎯⎯⎯⎯⎯
_____

3. a. I **walked** across a large meadow. (was walking) ⎯⎯⎯⎯
_____

   b. There **were many** flowers in bloom. (was a) ⎯⎯⎯⎯⎯
_____

   c. **The landscape** looked peaceful. (it) ⎯⎯⎯⎯⎯⎯⎯
_____

   d. **I was** in a hurry. (we) ⎯⎯⎯⎯⎯⎯⎯⎯⎯
_____

   e. I remained for a while. (we) ⎯⎯⎯⎯⎯⎯⎯⎯
_____

   f. **There** was **silence** around me. (it, silent) ⎯⎯⎯⎯⎯
_____

   g. That "buzzing" **I called** thought. (we call) ⎯⎯⎯⎯⎯
_____

4. a. There **were twenty-one children**. (was one) ⎯⎯⎯⎯⎯
_____

   b. **They were** very noisy. (I) ⎯⎯⎯⎯⎯⎯⎯⎯⎯
_____

   c. **One** small **boy was** from Indiana. (twenty-one) ⎯⎯⎯⎯
_____

   d. **I listened to him**. (they, me) ⎯⎯⎯⎯⎯⎯⎯⎯
_____

e. His father was an **attorney-at-law**. (teacher) _____

f. **The boy was** proud of **his** heritage. (we are) _____

5. a. The small boy confided in **a stranger**. (me) _____

b. Now it was **quiet** on the meadow. (peaceful) _____

c. People are **lonely**. (friendly) _____

d. **They** need someone to talk to. (we) _____

e. **We** must listen to children. (you) _____

f. We are called **thoughtful**. (considerate) _____

6. a. **A painter creates his** work in **his** thoughts. (painters) _____

b. **A person** can think before **he acts**. (I) _____

c. **People** commit fewer mistakes when **they** listen. (we) _____

d. Many misunderstandings **are** avoided. (can be) _____

III. Structures (Key words [phrases] for composition)

A. Use the following key words [phrases] to form complete sentences. You may consult the MODEL COMPOSITION.

Example: I think / I am
I think; therefore I am.

1. a. question / is / old and puzzling _____
   b. is / food / thought _____
   c. is / way / to encourage _____
2. a. are / many ways / thinking / stimulated _____
   b. are / productive / individuals _____

    c. study / English _____

    d. speak / create / thought_____

    e. write / think / English _____

    f. learning / one language / learning another / harder to progress _____

    _____

3. a. went / slowly and leisurely / across _____

    _____

    b. flowers / trees / were / in bloom _____

    c. landscape / was / inviting _____

    d. thoughts / readily / creative _____

    e. was / silence / around _____

    f. was / a special / buzzing _____

    g. buzzing / called / thought _____

4. a. were / twenty-one / on the meadow_____

    _____

    b. were / very / noisy _____

    c. boy / was / from / Indiana _____

    d. I listened / was / glad _____

    e. father / was / attorney-at-law _____

    f. boy / was / proud / heritage _____

5. a. wondered / boy / confided_____

    b. was / quiet / meadow _____

    c. was / present / to disturb _____

    d. people / are / lonely _____

    e. need / someone / to talk _____

    f. must / listen / children _____

    g. called / thoughtful / listen _____

6. a. not all / thinking / is_____

    b. painter / creates / work _____

    c. person / can think _____

    d. that kind / is called _____

    e. misunderstandings / are avoided _____

    f. type of thought / called / creative _____

    _____

g. are / not destructive / considered / creative _____

_____

B. Supply the missing **preposition** for each blank space. You may consult the MODEL COMPOSITION.

Example: ____(To)____ think, is ____(to)____ exist.

1. a. This is food _____ thought.

   b. It was a way _____ encourage thought.

2. a. There are many ways _____ which thinking is stimulated.

   b. We write and think only _____ English.

   c. Thinking _____ one language, but learning another, makes it harder _____ progress creatively.

3. a. I walked _____ a large meadow.

   b. There were many flowers _____ bloom.

   c. I was _____ a hurry.

   d. I remained _____ a while.

   e. Thoughts came _____ me readily.

   f. There was silence _____ me.

   g. There was a very special buzzing _____ my mind.

4. a. There were twenty-one children _____ the meadow.

   b. One boy was _____ Indiana.

   c. I listened _____ him.

   d. His grandfather took part _____ the Spanish-American War.

   e. The boy was proud _____ his heritage.

5. a. The boy confided _____ a stranger.

   b. It was quiet _____ the meadow.

   c. There was no one present _____ disturb me.

   d. People need someone _____ talk to.

   e. We must listen _____ children.

6. a. He creates his work _____ his mind.

   b. That kind _____ thought is called creative.

   c. In a manner _____ speaking, this type _____ thought is creative.

IV.   Grammar and Syntax [Points of Interest]

A.   Coordination and Coordinators

1. The COMPOUND SENTENCE has two or more full PREDICATIONS in the form of **independent clauses.** Each of the ideas expressed are closely related. The clauses are really two or more simple sentences joined together by connecting words (COORDINATORS) such as **and, but, for, nor, or, so** and **yet.**

2. COORDINATORS **and, but** and **or** serve to connect several grammatical units.

> Example: **Susan and I** are good students. (n.)
> Susan **reads and studies** her lesson. (v.)
> Susan is **pretty but shy.** (adj.)
> Susan calls me up **once or twice** a week. (adv.)

3. Expressions that indicate a definite relationship between stated ideas are connected frequently by the words **however, therefore, on the other hand, nevertheless, for example, consequently** or by a **semicolon (;).**

> Examples: Two **simple** sentences: The question is old.
> The question is not puzzling.
>
> **Compound** sentence: The question is old, but it is not puzzling.
>
> Two **simple** sentences: Thoughts came to me readily. I felt creative.
>
> **Compound** sentence: Thoughts came to me readily, and I felt creative.
>
> Two **simple** sentences: There was silence around me. There was a very special "buzzing" in my mind.
>
> **Compound** sentence: There was silence around me, but there was a very special "buzzing" in my mind.
>
> Two **simple** sentences: I listened to him. He was glad.
>
> **Compound** sentence: I listened to him, and he was glad.
>
> Three **simple** sentences: People are lonely. They need someone to talk to. They seldom listen.

Compound sentence:	People are lonely and they need someone to talk to, yet they seldom listen.
Three **simple** sentences:	There were twenty-one children on the meadow. They were noisy. One small boy was very quiet.
Compound sentence:	There were twenty-one children on the meadow and they were noisy, but one small boy was very quiet.

[NOTE: We must not leave out completely the punctuation mark or the coordinator. The coordinators can be used without a comma, but a comma may not be used without a coordinator.]

Wrong: I was in a hurry, not seeing anyone present, I remained for a while.

Correct: I was in a hurry, but not seeing anyone present, I remained for a while.

Wrong: There was silence around me, there was a very special "buzzing" in my mind.

Correct: There was silence around me, but there was a very special "buzzing" in my mind.

B.   Sentence Faults

1. Coordinators are used to join equal grammatical structures. This joining of grammatical structures is called PARALLELISM. It is an arrangement of **words, phrases, clauses** or **sentences** of similar or logically related ideas.

A correct parallel structure will relate a **noun** with a **noun**, an **infinitive** with another **infinitive**, an **adjective** with an **adjective**, etc.

Examples: They learn about the **origin** and **development** of meditation.

Susan likes **to study** and **to read.**

School has taught us **to encourage** thought and **to learn** by experience.

We **speak** and **create** new thoughts.

The children were very **noisy** and **playful.**

2. **Faulty Parrallelism** develops when **unparalleled** grammatical structures are joined into sentences.

Faulty Parallelism	*Corrected Parallelism*
Susan likes to study and reading.	Susan likes to study and to read.
I'm reading about thought and how it developed.	I'm reading about thought and its development.
Thinking on the meadow and to walk on it is a great pleasure.	Thinking and walking on the meadow is a great pleasure.
The boy was small, with brown hair, and who had a happy face.	The boy was small, brown-haired, and happy-faced.

C. Punctuation

1. The COMMA is followed by the coordinators **and, but, for, yet, or, nor** and **so** when it joins two (or more) main clauses in a COMPOUND SENTENCE.

> Examples: We study English, and we think in English.
> (2 main clauses)
>
> I listened to him, and he was glad.
> (2 main clauses)
>
> People are lonely, but they don't listen.
> (2 main clauses)
>
> They need someone to talk to, yet they seldom listen.
> (2 main clauses)

2. The SEMICOLON SEPARATES two independent clauses (COMPOUND SENTENCE) when a coordinator is not used.

> Examples: We are productive individuals; we think.
> I think; therefore I am.
>
> I wondered why the small boy confided in a stranger; I was a stranger to him.
>
> A person can simply think before he acts; that kind of thought is called "wisdom."

3. The HYPHEN is used here for the purpose of connecting.

a. **multiple numbers**: There were twenty-one children on the meadow.

b. **describing a profession**: His father was an attorney-at-law.

    c. connecting **adjectives** describing countries: His grandfather took part in the Spanish-American War.

D. Exercises

    1. The following sentences are incorrectly joined. Select one of the CO-ORDINATORS (and, but, for, nor, or, so, yet) to make the necessary correction.

        Example: We have a lot to read, we will need to hurry.
                    We have a lot to read, and we will need to hurry.

    a. The question is old, it is not puzzling. _____

_____

    b. Thoughts came to me readily, I felt creative. _____

_____

    c. There was silence around me, there was a very special "buzzing" in my mind. _____

_____

    d. I listened to him, he was glad._____

_____

    e. People are lonely, they need someone to talk to, they seldom listen.

_____

    f. There were twenty-one children on the meadow, they were noisy, one small boy was very quiet._____

_____

    g. I was in a hurry, not seeing anyone present, I remained for a while.

_____

    h. There was silence around me, there were twenty-one children on the meadow. _____

_____

    i. Thinking in one language, learning another, makes it harder to progress creatively. _____

_____

    j. A painter creates his work in his thoughts, does a writer, a dancer.

_____

    2. Transform the **simple** sentences into **compound** sentences. Make up simple sentences and add them on to those given below to form the compound sentences.

Example: I was in a hurry. **I did not see anyone.**
Compound: I was in a hurry, and I did not see anyone.

a. The question is old. _____

b. We see productive individuals. _____

c. We write compositions. _____

d. They think in one language. _____

e. She studies English. _____

f. I walked very slowly. _____

g. The landscape looked peaceful. _____

h. I was in a hurry. _____

i. Thoughts came to me readily. _____

j. There was silence around me. _____

k. I listened to the boy. _____

l. His father was an attorney-at-law. _____

m. It was quiet on the meadow. _____

n. People need someone to talk to. _____

o. We must listen to children. _____

p. We are called thoughtful. _____

q. A painter creates his work in his thought. _____

r. People think and listen. _____

s. Things are not destructive. —————————————————————

3. In the spaces provided below, write your own **compound** sentences. Follow the directions given before each group.

  a. Use a **comma** (,) and the coordinator "and."
   (1) —————————————————————————————
   (2) —————————————————————————————
  b. Use a **comma** (,) and the coordinator "but."
   (1) —————————————————————————————
   (2) —————————————————————————————
  c. Use a **comma** (,) and the coordinator "yet."
   (1) —————————————————————————————
   (2) —————————————————————————————

4. Correct the following sentences for FAULTY PARALLELISM. Write the corrected sentence in the space provided.

  a. Mike likes to think and to reading. —————————————

  b. We're learning about thought and how it developed. —————

  c. Thinking on the meadow and to walk on it is fun. ————

  d. Speaking and to create new thoughts is hard. —————

  e. He taught them to encourage thought and learning. ————

  f. Susan likes studying and to read.————————————

  g. The boy was small, with brown hair, and who had a happy face.

  h. To buy ads means selling products. ————————————

  i. He wanted to listen and playing with me. —————————

5. Punctuate the following passages. Use periods (.), question marks (?), exclamation marks (!), commas (,), semicolons(;) and hyphens (-) where they are necessary. The number on the right margin indicates how many corrections are needed.

What is thought What does it mean To be	2
productive individuals we must think Thinking in	2
one language but learning another makes it harder	2
to progress creatively When we study English we	2
must think in English	1
There were twenty one children on the meadow	1
One small boy was from Indiana the others were	1
Texans I wondered why the boy confided in	1
a stranger I was a stranger to him People are	2
lonely I thought They need someone yet they	3
seldom listen A person can think before he acts	2
that kind of thought is called "wisdom"	1

V. *Idea Recognition*

Copy from the MODEL COMPOSITION the sentences expressing:

A.   how old the question about thought is . . .

_____

B.   what explains the expression "food for thought" . . .

_____

C.   what the productive individual must do . . .

_____

D.   what we do when we study English . . .

_____

E.   what we must do when we study English . . .

_____

F.   the way thoughts came to the narrator . . .

_____

G.   the way the narrator felt . . .

_____

H.   what the narrator called "buzzing" . . .

_____

I.   why the narrator knew that the small boy was from Indiana . . .

_____

J.   what the people need . . .

_____

K.   what we must do with children . . .

_____

L.   what we are called when we listen . . .

_____

M.   what happens when people think and listen . . .

_____

N.   what things can be considered when they're not destructive . . .

VI.   Vocabulary Enrichment

A.   Paraphrasing

The following are **paraphrases** (rephrasing expressions or words without changing their meaning) of expressions or words found in the narrative. Write the expressions found in the MODEL COMPOSITION that correspond to the paraphrases below.

> Example: food for thought
> **things that stimulate meditation**

1. someone who thinks _____

2. someone who creates _____

3. difficult to continue creating _____

4. relax while walking _____

5. a pleasant countryside_____

6. pleased about one's past _____

7. he told the stranger about himself _____

8. no one likes to be alone_____

9. thinking means intelligence _____

B.   Lexical Units

Select the word (or phrase) from the following list that best completes each of the sentences below. You may use one selection more than once.

Example: I think; therefore I **am**.
         I think; therefore I **exist**.

stimulated	encourage	thought	progress
quiet	relax	quickly	talked readily
meditating	don't, often		

1. This is a way **to make you think**. It is a way to _____ .

2. Our **thinking grows** in many ways. Thinking is _____ in many ways.

3. Sometimes it is hard **to advance**. Learning one language, and thinking in another makes it hard to _____ .

4. He walked **slowly** and **leisurely**. He wanted to _____ .

5. The landscape looked **peaceful**. It was _____ .

6. He was in a **hurry**. He wanted to get somewhere _____ .

7. Thoughts came to him **readily**. His thinking was _____ .

8. There was a special **buzzing** in his mind. He called it _____ .

9. The small boy **confided** in a stranger. He _____ to him.

10. People are lonely. They **seldom** listen. They are lonely but they _____ listen.

C.   Related Words

Use the **related words** to rewrite the following sentences without changing their meanings. Change the underlined word. Make further changes if necessary.

Example: to think (v.)   thinking (n.)
         I **think**, therefore I am.
         Thinking is being.

puzzle (n.)	to encourage (v.)	to study (v.)
puzzling (adj.)	encouraging (adj.)	study (n.)
to think (v.)	leisure (n.)	studying (v.)
thought (n.)	leisurely (adv.)	

1. The question is **puzzling**. _____

2. It is a way to **encourage** thought. _____

3. **To study** English requires thought. _____

4. I walked **leisurely** across the meadow. _____

5. Not all **thinking** is creative. _____

VII. *Steps in Writing*

A.   Add new words and revise the sentence, if necessary, to suit the changes indicated in parentheses.

>   Example: **I** think; therefore I am. (he)
>   He **thinks**; therefore he is.

1. To be productive **individuals**, we must think. (individual)

_____

2. When **we** study English, **we** think. (he)

_____

3. **We** speak and create new thought. (One)

_____

4. **We write** and think only in English. (He speaks)

_____

5. **I walked slowly and leisurely** across a meadow. (He ran quickly)

_____

6. **I** was in a hurry. (We)

_____

7. Thoughts came to **me** readily. (her)

_____

8. There were **twenty-one** children on the meadow. (32)

_____

9. **The boy** was proud of **his** heritage. (We)

_____

10. **I** was a stranger to **him**. (They, us)

_____

11. **People** are lonely. (We)

_____

12. **They** seldom listen. (She)

_____

13. **We** must listen to children. (You)

_____

14. **A painter** creates **his** work in **his** thoughts. (Painters)

_____

15. **This** is creative thought. (Those)

_____

B. **Opposites**

Use the **opposites** to rewrite the following sentences. Make the necessary changes to suit the new sentences.

      Example: puzzling—clear
              The question is **puzzling**.
              The question is **clear**.

discourage	unproductive	regress	deadened	destructive
with effort	quickly	quiet	noisy	inconsiderate

1. This is a way to **encourage** thought. _____

_____

2. Our desires are **stimulated**. _____

_____

3. When we don't think, we are **productive**. _____

_____

4. Things that are unproductive are **creative**. _____

_____

5. When we are destructive, we **progress**. _____

_____

6. He walked **slowly**; he was in a hurry. _____

_____

7. He couldn't think; thoughts came **readily**. _____

_____

8. The children were peaceful. They were **loud**. _____

_____

9. It was **quiet** on the meadow. _____

_____

10. When we don't listen we are **considerate**. _____

_____

VIII. *Comprehension*

A. Complete the following sentences and add as many related sentences as you can find in the MODEL COMPOSITION.

> Example: The other day I heard someone say, **"This is food for thought."** **It was, perhaps, a way to encourage creative thought.**

1. There are many ways _____

2. When we study English, _____

3. Thinking in one language, but learning another, _____

4. Once I walked slowly and leisurely _____

5. I was in a hurry _____

6. Thoughts came to me readily, _____

7. I listened to the boy, _____

8. Now it was quiet _____

9. People are lonely, _____

10. A painter creates _____

11. But a person can simply think _____

12. When people think and listen _____

13. In a manner of speaking _____

14. Things that are not destructive, _____

B.   Answer each question with a complete sentence.

> Example: Why am I?
>   I am; because I think.

1. What is old and puzzling? _____

2. What was it the narrator heard someone say?_____

_____

3. Why must we think?_____

_____

4. When do we create new thoughts?_____

_____

5. When must we think in English?_____

_____

6. Where did the narrator walk?_____

_____

7. Why did the narrator remain on the meadow?_____

_____

8. How did the thoughts come to him?_____

_____

9. What was it the narrator called the "buzzing"?_____

_____

10. How many children were there on the meadow?_____

_____

11. Where did the small boy come from?_____

_____

12. Did the small boy know the narrator?_____

_____

13. What was the boy's father? Grandfather?_____

_____

14. Why was the boy glad?_____

_____

15. What do people need?_____

_____

16. Why must we listen to children?_____

_____

17. What do we call a considerate person?_____

_____

18. How does a painter create his work?_____

_____

19. When do people commit fewer mistakes?_____

_____

20. How is misunderstanding avoided?_____

_____

IX. *Commentary on Model*

A.   1. Tell what you learned about **thought** from section 2 of MODEL COM-POSITION.

2. Tell what you learned about **people** and **children** from paragraphs 4 and 5 of MODEL COMPOSITION.

3. Discuss why thinking is not always **creative**.

4. Give an appropriate title to your composition.

B.   1. Discuss the points in the MODEL COMPOSITION with which you agree.

2. Discuss the points in the MODEL COMPOSITION with which you disagree.

3. Tell in your own words what **you've** learned about creative thought.

4. Give an appropriate title to your composition.

X. *Composition*

A.   Using the following key words and phrases from the MODEL COMPOSI-TION, write your own composition on a related topic.

old and puzzling	food for thought	encourage creative thought
thinking is stimulated	speak and create	progress
meditation	peaceful and inviting	silence
children	people	lonely
considerate	listen	understand
wisdom	create	misunderstanding
mistake	destructive	creative

B.   1. Rewrite section 2 in the **I** person. Make all appropriate changes.

Example: There are many ways in which **my** thinking is stimulated.

2. Rewrite section 3 changing **I** to **Susan** and **Mark**. Make all appropriate changes.

Example: Once **Susan** and **Mark** walked slowly and leisurely across the meadow.

C. Describe briefly what you see in the picture below.

Chapter Four

The Complex Sentence

Words to remember:

Complex Sentence

Main = Independent Clause
Subordinate = Dependent Clause

Relationships
Subordination and Subordinators
(Clause Markers)

*Time (***after***) – Place (***where***) – Contrast*

*(***although***) – Condition (***although***)*

*Purpose (***in order that***) – Cause (***as***)*

*Manner and Comparison (***as though***)*

Comma (,) – Colon (:) – Quotation Marks (" ")

I. *Model Composition*

A. Love

1. Although much has been written about this subject, whenever we are puzzled about it, we ask the question: What is love? Love means different things to different people. Children regard love from their point of view, while they are very young. As we grow older, love grows into different dimensions with our maturing. Love changes constantly, because we change from day to day.

2. There are different kinds of love. Whereas we live in a mechanized world, we hold a special affection for nature. When you look at the lake, your heart is glad that the water is there. Unless you spend a week in the mountains, you will not know the beneficial effects of mountain air. As soon as the tidal sea wave touched your feet, you realized why you had always wanted to be at the seashore. My father used to say: "Man goes back to water, as though he had come from its depths."

3. Wherever there is a family, there is the love of a parent for the child. Warmth and support are basic needs. There is also the love of a child for its parent. Family love means being your natural self, in order that fear and deception vanish. For parents, it means caring for someone's needs more than for themselves. Before thinking of themselves, parents will help their children. Once you have found the need to be with someone, you will also feel the desire to share and to care. As long as man has existed, family love has been the cornerstone of civilized society.

4. When true love comes, you do not seek sensations, which are independent of one another and soon forgotten. You feel a lasting affection for each other, in that you long for one another. Two people unite into one. You want to give everything to the person you love. You're not afraid of death. Now that you've found love, you're only afraid that your loved one might die first.

5. The love between man and woman is strong, although at times it seems confusing. Whether it is a lasting bond, or simply the moment of the act of love, it leaves a deep feeling of joy and fulfillment. In love-making there is a complete giving of oneself to another person, since there is a unity of body and mind. This giving is truly unselfish, as it aims only at pleasing the other person.

6. Love has been called an "abstract" thing, which means that it is difficult to define. But for those who seek it, it is very real. They find comfort in the touch of a hand, or a kiss or being close to someone dear. Sick persons can become well again, as soon as love enters their hearts. Love can overcome family

feuds, it can bring together people of different ages, as well as ethnic and national backgrounds. Love brings people together, because they care.

B. Composition by Degrees

  1. a. Copy the title of the MODEL COMPOSITION.

     _____

     b. Copy the question we ask when we are puzzled.

     _____

     c. Copy the sentence that tells what love "means to different people."

     _____

     d. Copy the sentence that tells how "children regard" love.

     _____

     e. Copy the sentence that tells how "love changes."

     _____

  2. a. Copy the phrase that tells what we "hold" for nature.

     _____

     b. Copy the phrase that tells why your "heart is glad."

     _____

     c. Copy the sentence that tells about the mountains.

     _____

     d. Copy the sentence that tells you why man goes "back to water."

     _____

  3. a. Copy the sentence that tells about "warmth and support."

     _____

     b. Copy the sentence that tells about "parents' caring."

     _____

     c. Copy the sentence that tells about "parents helping their children."

     _____

     d. Copy the sentence that tells about the "desire to share and to care."

     _____

     e. Copy the sentence that tells about the "cornerstone of civilized society."

     _____

  4. a. Copy the sentence that tells what happens "when true love comes."

     _____

     b. Copy the phrase that tells what you "feel for each other."

     _____

   c. Copy the phrase that tells what "two people" do.

_____

   d. Copy the phrase that tells what you "want to give to the person you love."

_____

   e. Copy the sentence that tells about "death."

_____

5. a. Copy the sentence that tells about the "love between man and woman."

_____

   b. Copy the phrase that tells what "love leaves."

_____

   c. Copy the phrase that tells what there is in "love-making."

_____

   d. Copy the phrase that tells how the giving "truly is."

_____

6. a. Copy the phrase that tells what love has "been called."

_____

   b. Copy the sentence that tells for whom love is "very real."

_____

   c. Copy the sentence that tells what happens when "love enters their hearts."

_____

   d. Copy the phrases that tell what "love can overcome."

_____

II. Words in Context

A. From the list of words and phrases preceding each section fill in each blank space provided in the text. You may use a selection more than once. Also, you may use more than one word in one blank space.

1. subject	whenever	love	although
older	maturing	grow(s)	dimensions
while	point of view	different	

_____ much has been written about this_____ matter, _____
we are puzzled about it we ask the question: What is _____? _____
means_____ things to _____people. Children regard _____

from their _____ _____ they are very young. As we _____
older, _____ _____ into _____ with our _____ .

2. glad   as soon as   whereas   mechanized
   when   unless   as though   depths
   affection   beneficial   mountain(s)   touched

_____ we live in a _____ world, we hold a special _____
for nature. _____ you look at a lake, your heart is _____ that the
water is there. _____ you spend a week in the _____ you will not
know the _____ effects of _____ air. _____ the tidal sea wave
_____ your feet you realize why you had always wanted to be at the seashore. Man goes back to water, _____ he had come from its _____ .

3. in order that   family   before   wherever once
   child(ren)   care   parents   love   need
   share   as long as   cornerstone

_____ there is a _____ , there is the _____ of a parent
for the _____ . _____ means being your natural self, _____
fear and deception vanish. _____ thinking of themselves, _____ will
help their _____ . _____ you have found the _____ to be with
someone, you will also find the desire to _____ and to _____ .
_____ man has existed, _____ has been the _____ of civilized
society.

4. sensations   forgotten   when   love   independent
   in that   now that   afraid   affection

_____ true _____ comes, man does not seek _____ , which
are _____ of one another and soon _____ . You feel a lasting _____
for each other, _____ you search out one another. _____ you've
found love, you're only _____ that your loved one might die first.

5. confusing   as   complete   although   strong
   since   unselfish   unity   oneself

The love between man and woman is _____ , _____ at
times it seems _____ . In love-making there is a _____ giving of
_____ to another person, _____ there is a _____ of body and
mind. This giving is truly _____ , _____ it aims only at pleasing the
other person.

6. love   which   person(s)   abstract
   as soon as   heart(s)   define
   feuds   together   backgrounds

_____ has been called an _____thing, _____ means
that it is difficult to _____ . Sick _____can become well again,
_____ _____ enters their _____. _____ can overcome
family_____, it can bring_____ people of different ages, as well as
ethnic and national _____.

B.   Make any necessary changes when you substitute the new element into
your sentence.

   Example: Whenever **we are** puzzled about it, **we** ask the question. (I)
             Whenever **I am** puzzled about it, **I** ask the question.

1. a. Love means different things to different **people**. (men)

   _____

   b. **Children** regard love from **their** point of view. (we)

   _____

   c. As **we** grow older, love changes. (they)

   _____

   d. Love changes constantly because **we** change. (you)

   _____

2. a. Whereas **we** live in a mechanized world, **we** hold a special affection
      for nature. (she)

   _____

   b. When **you** look at a lake, **you are** happy. (I)

   _____

   c. Unless **you** spend a week in the mountains, **you** will not appreciate
      the mountain air. (we)

   _____

   d. **Man goes** back to water, as though **he** had come from its depths. (we)

   _____

3. a. Family love means being **your** natural self. (my)

   _____

   b. Before thinking of **themselves, parents** will help **their** children. (my-
      self, I, my)

   _____

c. As long as **man has** existed, family love has been the cornerstone of civilized society. (we)

_____

4. a. **You feel** a lasting affection. (she)

_____

b. **You** search out one another. (we)

_____

c. **Two people** unite into one. (they)

_____

d. **You** want to give everything to **the person you love**. (I, her)

_____

e. **You're not** afraid of death. (one is)

_____

5. a. The love between **man and woman** is strong. (them)

_____

b. It leaves a deep feeling of **joy**. (fulfillment)

_____

c. **There is a** unity of mind and body. (it results in)

_____

d. **It** aims at pleasing **the other person**. (she, him)

_____

6. a. **Love** is difficult to define. (it)

_____

b. **They** find comfort in the touch of a hand. (some people)

_____

c. Sick **persons** can become well again. (people)

_____

d. Love can overcome family **feuds**. (hatreds)

_____

e. Love **brings together** people of different nationalities. (unites)

_____

III. Structures (Key words [phrases] for composition)

A. Use the following key words [phrases] to form complete sentences. You may consult the MODEL COMPOSITION.

Example: much / been / about / subject matter
Much has been written about this subject matter.

1. a. love / means / different things _____

   _____

   b. regard / love / point of view _____

   _____

   c. love / changes _____

   _____

   d. we / change _____

   _____

2. a. are / kinds / of love _____

   _____

   b. hold / special / affection _____

   _____

   c. spend / week / in the mountains _____

   _____

   d. realize / you / wanted / seashore _____

   _____

   e. goes / to water _____

   _____

3. a. wherever / family / the love / parent / child _____

   _____

   b. are / basic _____

   _____

   c. is / love / child / parent _____

   _____

   d. means / being / natural /self _____

   _____

   e. caring / someone's / needs / more _____

   _____

   f. family / has been / cornerstone _____

   _____

4. a. feel / lasting / affection _____

   _____

   b. people / unite _____

   _____

   c. want / to give / the person _____

d. not / afraid / death _____

5. a. between / man and woman _____

b. leaves / deep feeling / joy_____

c. is / truly / unselfish _____

d. aims / pleasing / person _____

6. a. has been / called / abstract_____

b. is / difficult / define _____

c. seek / it / real _____

d. find / comfort / in the touch _____

e. can / become / well _____

f. overcome / feuds / bring / people / different / backgrounds _____

B. Supply the missing **subordinators (clause markers)** for each blank space. You may consult the MODEL COMPOSITION.

Example: __(Although)__ much has been written about love, we love.

1. a. _____ we are puzzled, we ask "what is love?"
   b. Some regard love from one point of view, _____they are very young.
   c. _____ we grow older, love grows with us.
2. a. _____ we live in cities, we hold an affection for nature.
   b. _____ you see a lake, you are happy.
   c. _____ you spend vacations in the mountains, you will not appreciate mountain air.
   d. _____ the water has touched your feet, you know why you love the seashore.

e. Man goes back to water, _____ he had come from its depths.

3. a. _____ there is a family, there is love.

b. It means being your natural self, _____ fear and deception vanish.

c. _____ thinking of themselves, parents will help their children.

d. _____ you have found the need to be with someone, you'll also feel the desire to share and care.

e. _____ man lives, love is important.

4. a. _____ true love comes, you feel happy.

b. You feel a lasting affection for each other, _____ you search out one another.

c. _____ you've found love, you're no longer afraid.

5. a. The love between man and woman is strong, _____ it seems confusing.

b. _____ it is a lasting bond, _____ simply the act of love, it leaves a deep feeling of joy.

c. There is a complete giving of oneself, _____there is a unity of body and mind.

d. Giving is truly unselfish, _____ it aims only at pleasing the other person.

6. a. Sick persons can become well again, _____ love enters their hearts.

b. Love brings people together, _____they care.

IV.   *Grammar and Syntax [Points of Interest]*

A.   Subordination and Subordinators

1. The COMPLEX SENTENCE has one main (independent) clause and one or more subordinate (dependent) clauses. The **main clause** contains a completely stated thought. The **subordinate** clause lacks the sense of completeness; for that reason, it is called the **dependent clause**.

The subordinate (dependent) clause depends on a main (independent) clause. The dependent clause is introduced by means of SUBORDINATORS (subordinate conjunctions). Since the subordinator is part of the clause it introduces, there is no need to separate it from its clause by a comma or any other punctuation mark.

The SUBORDINATORS (clause markers) show different RELATION-
SHIPS.

a. **Time Relationship**:

After we said goodbye, I went home.

As we grow older, love grows into different dimensions.

Before thinking of themselves, parents will help their children.

Now that love is here, you're happy.

Once you have found the need to be with someone, you will also feel the desire to share.

Until that day comes, there will be no happiness.

When you look at a lake, your heart is glad that the water is there.

Whenever we are puzzled about it, we ask the question.

Children regard love from their point of view, **while** they are very young.

As long as man has existed, family love has been the cornerstone of civilized society.

As soon as the tidal sea wave touched your feet, you realized why you had always wanted to be at the sea shore.

b. **Place Relationship**:

Where there is a will, there is a way.

Wherever there is a family, there is love of a parent for a child.

c. **Manner and Comparison**:

Man goes back to water, **as though** he had come from its depths.

d. **Contrast of Ideas**:

Although much has been written about this subject, we still ask the question: What is love?

Whereas we live in a mechanized world, we hold a special affection for nature.

e. **Condition**:

Unless you spend a week in the mountains, you will not know the beneficial effects of mountain air.

f. **Cause**:

Love changes constantly, **because** we change from day to day.

You feel a lasting affection for each other, **in that** you search out one another.

In love-making there is a complete giving of oneself, **since** there is a unity of body and mind.

g. **Purpose:**

We must grow older, **in order that** we may better understand love.

The following CLAUSE MARKERS were introduced in the MODEL COMPOSITION:

Time Relationship	— **after, before, now that, once, until, when, whenever, while, as soon as**
Place Relationship	— **where, wherever**
Manner and Comparison	— **as though**
Contrast of Ideas	— **although, whereas**
Condition	— **unless**
Cause	— **because, in that, since**

B.   Sentence Faults

1. Normally, English sentence order is SUBJECT, VERB AND COMPLE-MENT. MODIFIERS appear either before or after the word they modify. The modifier is placed as closely as possible to the word it modifies. When related parts of the sentence are unnecessarily split, the sentence is confusing and often misleading.

A modifier is called a "dangling modifier" when it has no word in a sentence to modify.

Example:

Walking into the hall, the air felt cooler.

In the above sentence, the writer took for granted that the reader would understand that somebody walked into the hall. But in the main clause, "the air felt cooler," the only noun is **air**. The air cannot walk into the hall. We could correct the sentence, by supplying the noun or the pronoun described by the **participial phrase:**

Corrected Example:

Walking into the hall, she felt the air grow cooler.

or
> **As she walked** into the hall, the air felt cooler.

2. When two **main clauses** are joined with a comma between them, the resulting sentence can be confusing. This is called **comma splice**.

> Examples of **comma splices**:
>> We are puzzled about it, we ask a question.
>>
>> We grow older, love grows into different dimensions.
>>
>> You spend a week in the mountains, you will not know the beneficial effects of mountain air.

The way to correct the **comma splice** sentence, is to **subordinate** one of the main clauses.

> Examples:

Comma splice	— We are puzzled about it, we ask a question.
Subordination	— **Whenever** we are puzzled about it, we ask a question.
Comma splice	— We grow older, love grows into different dimensions.
Subordination	— **As** we grow older, love grows into different dimensions.
Comma splice	— You spend a week in the mountains, you will not know the beneficial effects of mountain air.
Subordination	— Unless you spend a week in the mountains, you will not know the beneficial effects of mountain air.

C.   Punctuation

1. The COMMA (,) is generally considered an **interruption** to the flow of thought in a sentence. It is followed by the coordinators **and, but, for, yet, or, nor** and **so** when it joins two (or more) **main clauses** in a COMPOUND SENTENCE (Chapter Three).

The COMMA is used after a **dependent clause** beginning a sentence. When a dependent clause comes after the main clause, there is no comma.

> Examples:
>> Whereas we live in a mechanized world, we hold a special

affection for nature.

When you look at a lake, your heart is glad that the water is there.

Wherever there is a family, there is the love of a parent for the child.

Use a COMMA before the **subordinators as, because** and **for** to make the meaning clear.

Example:
Love brings people together, because they care.

2. The COLON (:) indicates that a **list** of **things follows**. It can also be used before direct **quotations**.

Examples:
Whenever we are puzzled about it, we ask the question: What is love? What is affection? What is feeling?

My father used to say: "Man goes back to water as though he had come from its depths."

3. The double QUOTATION MARKS (" ") are used **before** and **after** words or phrases uttered by someone else and quoted directly.

Example:
My father used to say: "Man goes to water, as though he had come from its depths."

D.   Exercises

1. The following sentences are incorrectly joined. Select one of the SUB-ORDINATORS given for each section to make the necessary correction.

Example:
The tidal wave touched my feet, I liked it. (when)
When the tidal wave touched my feet, I liked it.

a. once   now that   before   after
   whenever   until   when   as
   as long as   while   as soon as

(1) We said goodbye, I went home._____
_____

(2) We grow older, love grows into different dimensions. _____

(3) Thinking of themselves, parents will help their children. _____

(4) We are puzzled about it, we ask the question. _____

(5) Children regard love from their point of view, they are very young. _____

(6) Man has existed, family love has been the cornerstone of civilized society. _____

(7) The tidal sea wave touched your feet, you realize why you had always wanted to be at the sea shore. _____

(8) Love is here, you're happy. _____

(9) You have found the need to be with someone, you will also feel the desire to share. _____

(10) That day comes, there is no happiness. _____

(11) You look at a lake, your heart is glad that the water is there. __

b. as though   where   although   in that
   whereas   unless   because   wherever
   since   in order that

(1) We must grow older, we may better understand love. _____

(2) In love-making there is a complete giving of oneself, there is a unity of body and mind. _____

(3) There is a will, there is a way. _____

(4) There is a family, there is love of a parent for the child. _____

(5) Man goes back to water, he had come from its depths. _____

(6) Much has been written about this subject, we still ask the question: What is love? _____

(7) We live in a mechanized world, we hold a special affection for nature. _____

(8) You spend a week in the mountains, you will not know the beneficial effects of mountain air. _____

(9) Love changes constantly, we change from day to day. _____

(10) You feel a lasting affection for each other, you search out one another. _____

2. Complete the following expressions by adding either a **dependent** clause or an **independent** clause to make **complex** sentences.

Example:
Although much has been written about this subject matter, **whenever we are puzzled, we ask the question: What is love?**

a. Children regard love from their point of view, _____

b. Love changes constantly, _____

c. Whereas we live in a mechanized world, _____

d. When you look at a lake, _____

e. Unless you spend a week in the mountains, _____

f. As soon as the tidal wave touched your feet, _____

g. Man goes back to water, _____

h. Wherever there is a family, _____

i. Family love means being your natural self, ————————————

———————————————————————————

j. Before thinking of themselves, ——————————————

———————————————————————————

k. When true love comes, ———————————————

———————————————————————————

l. You feel a lasting affection for each other, ——————————

———————————————————————————

m. Now that you've found love, ——————————————

———————————————————————————

n. The love between man and woman is strong, ——————————

———————————————————————————

o. Whether it is a lasting bond, ——————————————

———————————————————————————

p. In love-making there is a complete giving of oneself to another person, ——————————————————

———————————————————————————

q. This giving is truly unselfish, ——————————————

———————————————————————————

r. Love has been called an "abstract" thing, ————————————

———————————————————————————

s. But for those who seek it, ———————————————

———————————————————————————

t. They find comfort in the touch of a hand, ————————————

———————————————————————————

u. Sick persons can become well again, —————————————

———————————————————————————

v. Love can overcome family feuds, ——————————————

———————————————————————————

w. Love brings people together, ——————————————

———————————————————————————

3. In the spaces provided below, write your own **complex** sentences. Follow the directions given before each group.

a. Use a comma (,) and the subordinator "after."

(1) ———————————————————————

(2) ———————————————————————

b. Use a comma (,) and the subordinator "where."

(1) _____

(2) _____

c. Use a comma (,) and the subordinator "although."

(1) _____

(2) _____

d. Use a comma (,) and the subordinator "as though."

(1) _____

(2) _____

e. Use a colon (:) and a direct quotation (" ").

(1) _____

(2) _____

4. Correct the following sentences for DANGLING MODIFIERS. Write the corrected sentence in the space provided.

Example:
Walking into the hall, the air felt cooler.
Walking into the hall, she felt the air grow cooler.

a. Singing a song, the place was much happier. _____
_____

b. Reaching maturity, my mother allowed me to go out on a date. ___
_____

c. Spending a week in the mountains, the home was more enjoyable. _
_____

d. Realizing the need for each other, the house was filled with love. __
_____

e. Looking out of the window, the landscape was beautiful. _____
_____

5. Punctuate the following passages. Use periods (.), commas (,), colons (:), dashes (-) and quotation marks (" ") where they are necessary. The number on the right margin indicates how many corrections are needed.

There are different kinds of love Whereas we live in a   1
mechanized world we hold a special affection for nature When   2
you look at a lake your heart is glad that the water is there   2

Unless you spend a week in the mountains you will not know the	1
beneficial effects of mountain air As soon as the tidal sea	1
wave touched your feet you realize why you had always wanted to	1
be at the seashore My father used to say Man goes back to	3
water as though he had come from its depths	3
The love between man and woman is strong although at times	1
it seems confusing Whether it is a lasting bond or simply the	2
moment of the act of love it leaves a deep feeling of joy and	1
fulfillment In love making there is a complete giving of	2
oneself to another person since there is a unity of body and	1
mind This giving is truly unselfish as it aims only at pleasing	2
the other person	1

V. *Idea Recognition*

Copy from the MODEL COMPOSITION the sentences expressing:

A. what we are puzzled about . . .

_____

B. what love means to different people . . .

_____

C. how children regard love . . .

_____

D. how love changes . . .

_____

E. what we hold for nature . . .

_____

F. why you realize the need to be at the sea shore . . .

_____

G. when there is a love of a parent for the child . . .

_____

H. what family love means . . .

_____

I. what parents will do before thinking of themselves . . .

_____

J. how long love has been the cornerstone of civilized society . . .

_____

K. what happens when true love comes . . .

_____

L.   what you want to give to the person you love . . .

_____

M.   how the love of man and woman is . . .

_____

N.   what kind of giving love truly is . . .

_____

O.   how love is for those who seek it . . .

_____

P.   what love can overcome . . .

_____

Q.   why love brings people together . . .

_____

VI.   *Vocabulary Enrichment*

A.   Paraphrasing

The following are **paraphrases** (rephrasing expressions or words without changing their meaning) of expressions or words found in the narrative. Write the expressions found in the MODEL COMPOSITION that correspond to the paraphrases below.

>   Example: children see love differently
>   **children regard love from their point of view**

1. with years, love changes _____

_____

2. we don't dislike nature _____

_____

3. mountain air is useful _____

_____

4. man is attracted to water _____

_____

5. family love has no falsehood _____

_____

6. parents are unselfish _____

_____

7. true love is not for the moment _____

_____

8. two people become one_____
   _____

9. love is giving and pleasing the other _____
   _____

10. love is stronger than disagreement _____
    _____

B. Lexical Units

Select the word (phrase) from the following list that best completes each of the sentences below. You may use one word more than once.

> Example: We are **puzzled** about love.
> Love is **mysterious**.

good	origin	unselfish	assurance	become
changes	deception	lasting	strong	natural

1. Love means **different** things to **different** peopie. Love _____ from one person to another.
2. We hold a **special affection** for nature. It is _____ for man to love his environment.
3. Mountain air has a **beneficial** effect on man. It is _____ to breathe in mountain air.
4. Man may have **come from** the water. Water may have been man's _____ .
5. In a family you can **be yourself**. There is no need for _____ .
6. Parents **care more for their children** than for themselves. They are _____ .
7. Family love has been a **cornerstone** of society. It makes society _____ .
8. True love is not a sensation to be **soon forgotten**. It is a_____ relationship.
9. Two people **unite** into one. They _____ one.
10. Giving in love aims at **pleasing the other person**. This giving is truly _____ .
11. Those who seek love, **find comfort** in the touch of a hand. They seek _____ in touching.

C. Related Words

Use the **related words** to rewrite the following sentences without changing their meanings. Change the underlined word. Make further changes if necessary.

Example: puzzle (n.)   puzzling (adj.)
      It's a **puzzle.**   It's **puzzling.**

to seek (v.)	to need (v.)	to love (v.)	to look (v.)
seeking (v.)	need (n.)	love (n.)	look (n.)
	needing (v.)	loving (v.)	looking (v.)

to grow (v.)
  growing (v.)

1. **To love** means wanting to touch. ⎯⎯⎯⎯⎯⎯⎯⎯

2. When **you look** at a lake, you're glad. ⎯⎯⎯⎯⎯⎯

3. While **you grow** older, you change. ⎯⎯⎯⎯⎯⎯

4. Not all **love** is lasting. ⎯⎯⎯⎯⎯⎯⎯⎯

5. To **seek** love, means to need it. ⎯⎯⎯⎯⎯⎯

VII. Steps in Composition

A. Add new words and revise the sentence, if necessary, to suit the changes indicated in parentheses.

Example: **It** is a lasting love. (mine)
      Mine is a lasting love.

1. **Love** means different things to different people. (loving)

2. **Children** regard love from **their** point of view. (we)

3. There are **different** kinds of love. (many)

4. We hold a special affection for **nature.** (our family)

5. He has always wanted to be **in the mountains**. (at the seashore)

_____

6. **Warmth** and **support** are basic needs. (love, affection)

_____

7. There is the love of **a child** for **its parents**. (parent, children)

_____

8. **They** care for someone's needs. (I)

_____

9. You feel the desire to **share**. (give)

_____

10. **You** feel a lasting affection for **each other**. (I, you)

_____

11. **Two people** unite into one. (we both)

_____

12. **You** want to give to the person **you** love. (we)

_____

13. **You're not** afraid of death. (no one is)

_____

14. The love between **man** and **woman** is strong. (parent, child)

_____

15. Love brings **people** together, because **they** care. (us, we)

_____

B.   Opposites

Use the **opposites** to rewrite the following sentences. Make any necessary changes to suit the new sentence.

        Example: question—answer
                 We ask a **question**.
                 We give an **answer**.

appear	strong	uncivilized	same	together
sick	unselfish	sad	comfort	natural

1. Love brings on **different** feelings. _____

_____

2. We live in a **civilized** world. _____

_____

3. My heart is **glad**. _____

_____

4. Love means being your **unnatural** self. _____

_____

5. Where there is no love, fear and deception **vanish**. _____

_____

6. The love between man and woman is **weak**. _____

_____

7. The giving in love is **selfish**. _____

_____

8. **Healthy** persons can become well again. _____

_____

9. They find **discomfort** in the touch of a hand. _____

_____

10. Love can bring **apart** people of different ages. _____

_____

VIII. Comprehension

A. Complete the sentence and add as many related sentences as you can find in the MODEL COMPOSITION.

> Example: Although much has been written about this subject matter, **whenever we are puzzled, we ask the question: What is love?**

1. Love means different things _____

_____

2. Children regard love from their point of view, _____

_____

3. Whereas we live in a mechanized world, _____

_____

4. Wherever there is a family, _____

_____

5. Once you have found the need to be with someone, _____

_____

6. When true love comes, _____

_____

7. The love between man and woman is strong, _____

8. In love-making _____

9. Love has been called an "abstract" thing _____

10. Sick persons can become well again, _____

11. Love brings people together, _____

B.   Answer each of the following questions with a complete sentence.

    Example: What are we puzzled about?
       We're puzzled about love.

1. How do children regard love? _____

2. Why does love change constantly? _____

3. What do we hold for nature? _____

4. Why does man go back to water? _____

5. What are the basic needs? _____

6. What does family love mean? _____

7. When will parents help their children? _____

8. How long has family love been the cornerstone of civilized society?___

9. What happens when true love comes?_____

10. What kind of affection do people in love feel for each other? _____

11. Why do you want to give everything to the person you love? _____

12. What are you not afraid of? _____

13. What are you afraid of? _____

14. How is the love between man and woman? _____

15. What happens in love-making? _____

16. Why has love been called "abstract"? _____

17. What is love for those who seek it? _____

18. Who can become well again in love? _____

19. Whom does love bring together? Why? _____

IX. Commentary on Model

A.   1. Tell what you learned about the **family** from section 3 of the MODEL COMPOSITION.

2. Tell what you learned about **true love** from section 4.

3. Discuss why love is **puzzling**.

4. Give an appropriate title to your composition.

B.   1. Discuss the points in the MODEL COMPOSITION with which you agree.

2. Discuss the points in the MODEL COMPOSITION with which you disagree.

3. Tell in your own words what you've learned about love.

4. Give an appropriate title to your composition.

X. Composition

A. Using the key words and phrases from the MODEL COMPOSITION, write your own composition on a related topic.

love	people grow older	changes constantly
different kinds	affection for nature	mountain air
family love	parents and children	true love
man and woman	love-making	give everything
truly unselfish	comfort	touch
together	care	kiss

B. Rewrite section 4 of the MODEL COMPOSITION changing **you** to **I**.

Example: When true love comes, **I** do not seek sensations, etc.

C. Describe briefly what you see in the picture below.

Chapter Five

Logical or Natural Sequence of Tenses

Words to Remember:

after	*in (year)*
always	*later*
at birth, in childhood, etc.	*now*
at last	*nowadays*
at the turn of the	*next*
(century, decade, etc.)	
before	*previously*
during	*prior to*
earlier	*since*
every (number) (moment,	*soon*
year, month, day, etc.)	
finally	*then*
formerly	*when*
frequently	*while*

I.   Model Composition

A.   Remembrance

1. The street on which the Axbys now live is called Shadywood. It is called Shadywood because there are many shade trees there. Prior to moving there, the Axbys lived on Blanco Street. Mr. Axby is a school teacher and a widower. Mrs. Axby died during the past summer after a long illness. The children go to neighborhood schools. Ralph is the oldest and the tallest at the age of seventeen. He attends Meridian High School and plays tennis on the team. His brother John is a freshman at the same school. John loves to study and to read. Their sister Dorothy is in the eighth grade. She loves studying but not reading. She is in a habit of reading rapidly but is unable to learn well.

2. Dorothy was ill last week, but she is feeling better now. She stayed in bed several days, but she is doing some chores around the house today. She vacuums her room every day and prepares her clothing for the next day. Her father went to town earlier in the day and bought Dorothy a new dress. She was happy and tried it on right away.

3. Mr. Axby often waits in the car while his children come out of school. This happens only on days when it rains. Mrs. Axby used to attend to this chore in her lifetime. At times there is too much traffic, and Mr. Axby cannot find a place to park. When this happens, he drives many times around the block. The siblings are worried, but their father arrives as soon as the space is available.

4. Once every week the Axbys go to the cemetery and place flowers on Mrs. Axby's grave. While they stand at the graveside, they remember the good times. Mrs. Axby always told them to remember her and to be happy. Nowadays, they miss her cheerful personality. She was always happy and resourceful. The day always ends with a long hike after they leave for home. The Axbys remember and cherish their memories. It is important to remember our loved ones.

B.   Composition by Degrees

1. a. Copy the title of the MODEL COMPOSITION. _____

   _____

   b. What does the title tell you? The title tells that the composition is about _____

   _____

   c. Copy the name of the street on which the Axbys live. _____

d. Why is the street called by its name? Because there are many _____

e. Copy the word in paragraph 1 that says that Mr. Axby has no wife.

f. Copy the word in paragraph 1 that expresses "brothers and sisters."

g. Copy the name of the high school attended by the two brothers. __

h. Copy the word in paragraph 1 that says that Dorothy cannot learn well. _____

2. a. Copy the sentence that explains why Dorothy stayed in bed several days. _____

b. Copy the phrase that tells why Dorothy can do some chores around the house. _____

c. Copy the sentence that tells why Dorothy was happy. _____

3. a. Copy the phrase that tells why Mr. Axby waits in the car. _____

b. Copy the phrase that tells when Mr. Axby waits for his children.___

c. Copy the phrase that explains why Mr. Axby drives around the block. _____

d. Copy the phrase that tells how soon the father arrives. _____

4. a. Copy the phrase that tells how often the Axbys go to the cemetery.

b. Copy the reason for which the Axbys go to the cemetery. _____

c. Copy the phrase that tells where the Axbys stand. _____

d. Copy the phrase that tells what the Axbys remember._____

e. Copy the phrase that tells about Mrs. Axby's personality. _____

f. Copy the phrase that tells when the Axbys go on a hike. _____

II. Words in Context

A. From the list of words and phrases preceding each section fill in each blank space provided in the text. You may use a selection more than once. Also, you may use more than one word in one blank space.

1. live   died   does
    is called   has   loves
    are   go   read
    is   moving   to read
    reading   attends   studying
    learn   to study

The street on which the Axbys now_____ is called Shadywood. It ___ _____ Shadywood because there _____ many shade trees there. Prior to _____ there, the Axbys _____ on Blanco Street. Mr. Axby_____a school teacher and a widower. Mrs. Axby _____ during the past summer after a long illness. Mr. Axby _____ three children who_____ still of school age. The siblings _____ to neighborhood schools. Ralph _____ the oldest and the tallest at the age of seventeen. He_____Meridian High School and _____ well in school. John_____ _____ and _____ _____. Their sister Dorothy _____ in the eighth grade. She _____ _____but not_____. She _____ in the habit of _____ rapidly but unable _____ _____well.

2. several   next   last   feeling
    around   new   some   today
    happy   now   every
    right away   other   earlier

Dorothy was ill_____week, but she is _____better_____. She stayed in bed_____days, but she is doing _____chores_____the house _____. She vacuums her room _____ day and prepares her clothing for the _____ day. Her father went to town_____ in the day and bought Dorothy a _____ dress. She was_____and tried it on_____ _____.

3. siblings   car   children
    school   block   space
    traffic   father   place
    days

Mr. Axby waits in the _____ while his _____ come out of _____ . This happens only on_____when it rains. At times there is too much _____ and Mr. Axby cannot find a _____to park. When this happens, he drives many times around the_____. The _____ are worried, but their _____ arrives as soon as the _____ is available.

4.

at	to the cemetery	miss
at the	stand	usually
remember	happy	while
cheerful	resourceful	grave
after	recall	nowadays
always	graveside	cherish
every	memories	long

_____ year the Axbys go _____ _____ _____ and place flowers on Mrs. Axby's_____. _____ they stand_____ _____graveside, they _____ the good times. Mrs. Axby always told them to_____ her and reminded them to be _____. _____ , they_____ her _____ personality. She was _____ _____and _____. The day _____ ends with a long hike _____ they leave for home. The Axbys remember and _____their _____ .

B.   Make the necessary change(s) when you substitute the new element into your sentence.

> Example: **The Axbys** live on Shadywood street. (Ralph)
> Ralph **lives** on Shadywood street.

1. **The siblings** go to the neighborhood school. (Dorothy)

_____

2. Mr. Axby has **three** children. (one)

_____

3. **He attends** Meridian High. (They)

_____

4. **He** does well in school. (We)

_____

5. **John** loves to study and to read. (I)

_____

6. **She** loves studying but not reading. (They)

_____

7. **She** is in a habit of reading rapidly. (I)

_____

8. **Dorothy** was ill all of last week. (We)

_____

9. **She** is doing some chores around the house. (Ralph and Susan)

_____

10. **She** vacuums her room. (They)

_____

11. **He** prepares his clothing. (We)

_____

C. Replace each underlined **noun** or **phrase** with an appropriate **pronoun**. Change the sentence structure where necessary.

Example: **Mr. Axby** has three children.
He has three children.

1. **Dorothy** was ill last week. _____

_____

2. She vacuums **her room** every day. _____

_____

3. **Her father** went to town the other day. _____

_____

4. He bought **Dorothy** a new dress. _____

_____

5. She tried on the **dress** right away. _____

_____

6. Mr. Axby often waits in the car while **his children** come out of school.

_____

7. **The children** are worried. _____

_____

8. **Their father** arrives as soon as **the space** is available. _____

_____

D. Change the subjects from singular to plural and make the necessary changes.

Example: **He waits** in the car. (they)
They wait in cars.

1. **She** places flowers on Mrs. Axby's grave. (They)

_____

2. **He** stands at the graveside. (we)

_____

3. **She** remembers the good times. (they)

_____

4. Nowadays, **he** misses her cheerful personality. (we)

_____

5. **I** was always happy and resourceful. (we)

_____

6. The **day** always ends with a long hike. (days)

_____

7. **I** remember and cherish **my** memories. (They, their)

_____

III. Structures (Key words [phrases] for composition)

A.   Use the following key words [phrases] to form complete sentences. You may consult the MODEL COMPOSITION.

> Example: street / live
> **The Axbys now live on Shadywood Street.**

1. street / live / is called _____

_____

2. there are / shade trees _____

_____

3. is / a teacher / a widower _____

_____

4. died / after / illness _____

_____

5. has / children / still of school age _____

_____

6. the children / go _____

_____

7. is / oldest / tallest _____

_____

8. attends / does well _____

9. his brother / freshman / same school _____

10. loves / study / read _____

11. sister / is / eighth grade _____

12. studying / reading _____

B. Supply the missing **prepositions** for each blank space.

   Example: Use key words __(to)__ form complete sentences.

1. The street _____which the Axbys now live is called Shadywood.
2. Prior _____ moving there, the Axbys lived _____Blanco Street.
3. Mrs. Axby died _____ a long illness.
4. Three children are _____school age.
5. The siblings go_____neighborhood schools.
6. He is the tallest_____the age of seventeen.
7. John is a freshman _____ the same school.
8. He loves _____ study and_____read.
9. Their sister is_____the eighth grade.
10. She is _____ a habit _____ reading rapidly but is unable _____ learn well.
11. She stayed _____ bed several days.
12. She is doing some chores _____ the house now.
13. They prepare their clothing _____ the next day.
14. Her father went _____ town.
15. She tried _____ the dress right away.
16. Mr. Axby waits_____the car_____his children come _____ school.
17. This happens _____days when it rains.
18. _____ times there is too much traffic.
19. He cannot find a place _____ park.
20. The Axbys go_____the cemetery.

21. They place flowers _____ Mrs. Axby's grave.

22. He stands _____ the graveside.

23. She told them _____ remember and _____ be happy.

24. They go hiking after they leave _____ home.

C.   Complete the following sentences.

Example: The street on which Ralph lives **is called Shadywood.**

1. It is called Shadywood because there _____

_____ .

2. Dorothy was ill during last week, but _____

_____ .

3. Her father went to town earlier in the day and _____

_____ .

4. She was happy and _____

_____ .

5. Though times were often hard, she _____

_____ .

6. Mr. Axby often waits in the car _____

_____ .

7. The Axbys go to the cemetery _____

_____ .

8. They remember the good times _____

_____ .

9. They miss her cheerful personality _____

_____ .

10. The day always ends with a long hike _____

_____ .

IV.   Grammar and Syntax [Points Of Interest]

A.   Comments and Model Samples

1. VERB TENSE

Tense signifies the different verb forms which indicate the **difference of time.** There are six such tenses in English.

a. **Present** and **Present Progressive** indicate

    (1) an action going on or a condition existing **now.**

        Examples: Ralph **lives** on Shadywood Street.
                 Dorothy **is learning** her lesson.

    (2) a customary or general action (with such added words as **frequently, every day, always,** etc.).

        Examples: The children **go** to school every day.
                 They always **do** their homework.

b. **Simple Past** and **Past Progressive** indicate

    (1) that action took place or existed in some definite time in the past.

        Examples: She **was** happy and she **smiled.**
                 They **ate** their breakfast this morning.

    (2) that action took place or continued at some particular time in the past when something else happened.

        Examples: She **was studying** when her father came in.
                 While they **were driving** to school, they saw their teacher.

c. **Future** indicates an action that will take place or will exist.

        Examples: They **will visit** us next year.
                 They **visit** us next year.
                 They **are visiting** us next year.
                 They **shall be visiting** us next year.
                 They **are going to visit** us next year.

d. **Present Perfect Tense** indicates

    (1) that an action began in the past and continues to the present (connects the past to the present).

        Examples: She **has encouraged (has been encouraging)** Dorothy to study English for several years.

Dorothy **has worked (has been working)** hard since last week.

(2) that an action happened in an indefinite time in the past. The time of action is neither expressed nor implied.

Examples: They **have visited** the cemetery.
Have you ever **vacuumed** a room?
She **has vacuumed** her room already.

(3) that an action was repeated several times in an indefinite past.

Examples: We **have visited** her often.
He **has picked** them up time and again.

e. **Past Perfect Tense** expresses an action or condition completed before a certain time in the past or before another past action.

Examples: We **had left** before they **arrived**.
She **got** out of bed after the doctor **had given** her the injection.

f. **Future Perfect** tells of an action that began in the past and is to be completed at a future time **before** another future action will take place.

Examples: By Friday next week **we shall have finished** the chapter.
Dorothy **will have gotten** well before next Monday.
They'll **have learned** to study before they finish the course.

2. SEQUENCE OF TENSES

In the speaker's mind, the time an action takes place depends on how it relates to the time of speaking. For example, if the speaker says, "I bought Dorothy a new dress today," the time he **purchased** the dress is **past** in his mind. The verb **bought** is in the simple past. It expresses action **completed** in the past.

a. Coordination in a sentence means that the sentence is well **balanced**, it expresses concepts of equality, and it contains **parallel** structures (**parallelism**). Some examples of balanced sentences are:

(1) **Verb** with **verb**:
He loves **to study and to read.**

He loves **to study but** not **to read.**
He probably loves **either to study or to read.**
She loves **studying and reading.**
She loves **studying but** not **reading.**
She probably loves **either studying or reading.**

(2) **Adjective** with **adjective**:
He is the **oldest** and **tallest.**
Dorothy was **happy** and **resourceful.**
Ralph has a **younger** sister and **smaller** brother.

(3) **Adverb** with **adverb**:
She is in a habit of reading **rapidly** without learning **well.**
Although he drives **fast** he does it **well.**

b. LOGICAL or NATURAL SEQUENCE in a sentence means using tenses that naturally, or logically, follow a sequence in describing some activities. Events logically precede or succeed one another and have to be placed in their proper order in time. It is not logical, or natural, to say, "Her father **went** to town earlier in the day and **buy** Dorothy a new dress." The logical, or natural, sequence is "Her father **went** to town earlier in the day and **bought** Dorothy a new dress." Some examples of logical sequence follow:

(1) **Present** with **Present** (action takes place at the same time):
Mr. Axby **has** three children who **are** still of school age.
Mr. Axby often **waits** in the car while his children **come out** of school.
He seldom **waits** until I **come.**
At times there **is** too much traffic, and he cannot **find** a place to park.
But this **happens** only on days when it **rains.**
When this **happens**, he **drives** many times around the block.
The siblings **are** worried, but their father **comes** as soon as the space **is** available.
Every year the Axbys **go** to the cemetery and **place** flowers on Mrs. Axby's grave.
While they **stand** at the graveside, they **remember** the good times.
They **do**, but they **miss** her cheerful personality.
The Axbys **are** a closely knit family, and that **is** why they **miss** the departed Mrs. Axby.
The Axbys **remember** and **cherish** their memories.

(2) **Present Habitual** (action takes place as a consequence of another

action in the present):

The street on which Ralph **lives is called** Shadywood.

It **is called** Shadywood because **there** are many shade trees there.

I often **wait** until she comes.

Dorothy usually **waits** until we come.

They usually **recall** the past while they **are standing** at the grave-side.

The day always **ends** with a long hike as soon as they **leave** for home.

(3) **Past** with **Present** (action does not take place at the same time):

Dorothy **was** ill all of last week, but she **is feeling** better today.

She **stayed** in bed several days, but she **is doing** some chores around the house now.

She **vacuumed** her room yesterday; now she **is preparing** her clothing for the next day.

(4) **Past** with **Past** (action takes place at the same time):

She **was** happy and **tried** it on right away.

Mrs. Axby always **told** them to remember her, and **reminded** them to be happy.

Though times **were** often hard, she never **complained**.

c. Time sequence of tenses other than those discussed already follows similar logic. Below are some samples of logical or natural sequence in varied tense combinations.

(1) **Past** with **Present** and **Future**:

Dorothy **was** ill last week, she **is feeling** better today, and she **will be** in school tomorrow.

Mr. Axby **went** to town yesterday, but he **is staying** home today, and **he'll go** to town again on Tuesday.

(2) **Past Perfect** with **Past**:

The siblings **had left** before their father **came**.

Dorothy **went** to town after she **had received** some money.

(3) **Present** with **Future Perfect**:

Before she **vacuums** her room Dorothy **will have prepared** her clothing for the next day.

When their father **arrives**, the siblings **will have waited** a long time.

d. Logical sequence may also come as a result of various **clause** constructions. Examples:

(1) NOUN CLAUSE:
He **says** that he **studies** at Meridian High.
He **says** that he **studied** at Meridian High.
He **says** that he **will study** at Meridian High.
He **says** that he **has studied (has been studying)** at Meridian High.
He **said** that he **studies** at Meridian High. (never **studies**)
He **said** that he **would study** at Meridian High. (never **will study**)
He **said** that he **had studied** at Meridian High. (never **has studied**)

(2) ADVERBIAL CLAUSE: An adverbial clause modifies a verb.

(a) Main verb in the **present tense**:
A good student does not quit **as soon as his teacher leaves.**
while others are studying.
before he has finished his work.
until he has finished his work.

(b) Main verb in the **past tense**:
The children waited **until their father came.**
after they finished school.

(c) Main verb in the **future tense**:
They'll wait **until the traffic lets up.**
while Mr. Axby's getting ready.
until Ralph has finished his game.

(d) Main verb in the **past progressive tense**:
The children were waiting **when Mr. Axby got there.**
while Ralph was playing tennis.

(e) Main verb in the **present perfect tense**:
They have recalled the past **since Mrs. Axby died, because Mrs. Axby has asked them to.**
so that they will be able to cherish their memories.

(3) ADJECTIVAL CLAUSE: An adjectival clause modifies a noun and is not necessarily related to the action expressed by the verb. It involves a different concept of time in the mind of the speaker.

(a) The Ralph **that I know** attends Meridian High.
                            played tennis last Monday.

(b) The dress **that he bought** yesterday is in the closet.
                                was too long.

(c) Last night **I waited for the man** who was remembered by
                                my children.
                                who will be our neighbor.
                                who is considered a good
                                teacher.

B.   Exercises

1. Write the appropriate **present tense** form of the verb in parentheses:

   a. The street on which Ralph _____ (to live) is called Shadywood.

   b. It _____ (to be called) Shadywood because there _____ (to be)
   many shade trees there.

   c. Mr. Axby _____ (to have) three children who _____ (to be) still
   of school age.

   d. Ralph _____ (to have) a brother and a sister.

   e. He _____ (to attend) Meridian high school and _____ (to play)
   tennis on the team.

2. Change the above to the **past tense.**

3. Write the appropriate **past tense** form of the verb in parentheses:

   a. Ralph _____ (to go) to school at 7:30 this morning.

   b. Dorothy _____ (to be) ill yesterday.

   c. She _____ (to stay) in bed several days.

   d. Her father _____ (to go) to town the other day.

   e. He _____ (to buy) Dorothy a new dress.

4. Insert the correct form of the verb in parentheses:

   a. Dorothy _____ (to be) ill during last week, she _____ (to be)
   feeling better now, and she _____ (to be) in school tomorrow.

   b. Mr. Axby _____ (to go) to town yesterday, but he _____ (to
   be, to stay) home today, and he _____ (to go) to town again

on Tuesday.

c. The children _____ _____ (to have, to leave) before their father _____ (to come).

d. Dorothy _____ (to go) to town after she _____ _____ (to have, to receive) some money.

e. Before she _____ (to vacuum) her room, Dorothy _____ _____ (to have, to prepare) her clothing for the next day.

f. When their father _____(to arrive), the siblings _____ _____ (to have, to wait) a long time.

V.   *Idea Recognition*

A.   Copy from the MODEL COMPOSITION the sentences expressing:

1. where the Axbys live . . .

_____

2. why Mr. Axby is a widower . . .

_____

3. why John is a good student . . .

_____

4. why his sister Dorothy is not as good a student as John . . .

_____

5. why Dorothy stayed in bed . . .

_____

6. why Dorothy was happy . . .

_____

7. what happens when it rains . . .

_____

8. what happens when there is much traffic . . .

_____

9. why the children are worried . . .

_____

10. why the Axbys remember the good times . . .

_____

11. how Mrs. Axby was . . .

_____

12. who the Axbys miss . . .

_____

13. how the day ends . . .

_____

14. about the Axbys' memories . . .

_____

B.   Describe what is **happening** in relation to the following general statements according to the MODEL COMPOSITION. Write as many new sentences as you think possible.

> Example: **The street is called Shadywood.**
> **Ralph lives on Shadywood street.**
> **There are many shady trees on Shadywood street.**

1. Mrs. Axby died. _____

_____

_____

2. There are three children. _____

_____

_____

3. Ralph is seventeen years of age. _____

_____

_____

4. John is a good student. _____

_____

_____

5. Dorothy is not as good a student as John. _____

_____

_____

6. Dorothy was ill. _____

_____

_____

7. She stayed in bed. _____

_____

_____

8. Her father bought Dorothy a dress. _____

_____

_____

9. The children come out of school. _____

_____

_____

10. It rains. _____

_____

_____

11. There is too much traffic. _____

_____

_____

12. There are flowers on the grave. _____

_____

_____

13. They remember the good times. _____

_____

_____

14. Mrs. Axby was happy. _____

_____

_____

VI. *Vocabulary Enrichment*

A. Paraphrasing

The following are **paraphrases** (rephrasing expressions or words without changing their meaning) of expressions or words found in the narrative. Write the expressions found in the MODEL COMPOSITION that correspond to the paraphrases below.

> Example: a street called Shadywood
> **It is a place with many shade trees.**

1. man whose wife died _____

2. brothers and sisters _____

3. a tennis player _____

4. first-year student _____

5. an habitual reader _____

6. a rainy day _____

7. a parking place _____

8. at the graveside _____

9. a happy person _____

10. a long walk _____

B.   Lexical Units

Select the word (or phrase) from the following list that best completes each of the sentences below. You may use one selection more than once.

Example: This lesson is **easy**. The words are **not difficult.**

nearby	to leave	called
quick	rainy weather	parking place
is busy	dead	illness
purchase		

1. The **name** of the street is Shadywood. It is＿＿＿＿ Shadywood Street.

2. Mrs. Axby **died** after a long illness. She has been ＿＿＿＿＿ since the past summer.

3. The children go to **neighborhood** schools. They go to ＿＿＿＿ schools.

4. She is in a habit of reading **rapidly**. She is a ＿＿＿＿＿reader.

5. Dorothy was **ill** during last week. Her ＿＿＿ lasted one week.

6. She is **doing** some **chores** around the house. She＿＿＿＿ around the house.

7. Her father **bought** Dorothy a new dress. He went to town to ＿＿＿＿ a dress for Dorothy.

8. Mr. Axby waits until his children **come out** of school. He waits for his children ＿＿＿ ＿＿＿school.

9. This happens on **days when it rains**. It happens during＿＿＿ ＿＿＿ .

10. Mr. Axby cannot find a **place to park**. He cannot find a＿＿＿ ＿＿＿ .

C.   Related Words

Use the **related words** to rewrite the following sentences without changing their meaning. Change the underlined word. Make further changes if necessary.

Example: love (n.)   to love (v.)
          Dorothy **loves** studying.
          Dorothy has a love for studying.

to play (v.)	rapid (adj.)	to read (v.)
playing (v.)	rapidly (adv.)	reading (n.)
		reader (n.)
hike (n.)	shade (n.)	habit (n.)

hiking (v.)   shady (adj.)   habitual (adj.)
                                                     habitually (adv.)
to study (v.)   to park (v.)
studying (n.)   parking (n.)

1. Ralph **plays** tennis on the team. _____
_____

2. The trees provide a lot of **shade.** _____
_____

3. She is in a **habit** of **reading.** _____
_____

4. He loves to **study** and to **read.** _____
_____

5. He is a **rapid reader.** _____
_____

6. They all go on a **hike.** _____
_____

7. Mr. Axby can find a place to **park.** _____
_____

VII. Steps to Writing

A.   Add new words and revise the sentence, if necessary, to suit the changes indicated in parentheses.

> Example: She reads rapidly. (we)
>   We **read** rapidly.

1. **The Axbys** live on Shadywood Street. (she)
_____

2. **The children** go to neighborhood schools. (all of us)
_____

3. **Ralph** plays tennis on the team. (Dorothy and John don't)
_____

4. **John** loves to study and to read. (we don't always)
_____

5. **She** is in a habit of reading rapidly. (most people)
_____

6. **She** is doing some chores around the house. (they)

7. **Dorothy vacuums** her room and prepares her clothing. (we vacuumed)

8. **Her father** went to town and bought her a dress. (they will go)

9. **She** was happy and tried it on right away. (we)

10. This happens only on days **when it rains**. (rainy)

11. When they **stand** at the graveside, they remember the good times. (are standing)

B.   Opposites

Use the **opposites** to rewrite the following sentences. Make the necessary changes to suit the new sentence.

> Example: bachelor—married man
> Mr. Rowan is a **bachelor**.
> He is a married man.

bright	youngest	not feeling well	does not like	student
slowly	looks for	composed	displeased	unhappy

1. The street is very **shady**. _____

2. Mr. Axby is a **teacher**. _____

3. Mrs. Axby was **okay** for a long time. _____

4. Ralph is the **oldest** of the children. _____

5. John **likes** to study and to read. _____

6. She is in a habit of reading **rapidly**. _____

7. Dorothy was **happy** during last week. _____

8. She was **pleased** when she tried on the dress. _____

9. Mr. Axby **does not look** for a place to park. _____

10. The children are **worried.** _____

VIII.   Comprehension

A.   Complete the sentence and add as many related sentences as you can find in the MODEL COMPOSITION.

> Example: The street on which the Axbys live is called **Shadywood. It is called Shadywood because there are many shade trees there.**

1. Mr. Axby is a school teacher _____

2. She loves studying _____

3. Dorothy was ill during last week _____

4. Mr. Axby often waits in the car _____

5. Every week the Axbys go to the cemetery _____

B.   Answer each question with a complete sentence.

> Example: Why is the street called Shadywood?
> **It is called Shadywood Street because there are many shade trees there.**

1. When did Mr. Axby become a widower? _____

2. Why is John a good student? _____

3. Why isn't Dorothy able to learn well? _____

4. How long did Dorothy stay in bed? _____

5. Why is she doing some chores around the house? _____

6. For what occasion did Dorothy's father go to town?_____

7. What made Dorothy happy?_____

8. When does Mr. Axby come to wait for his children? _____

9. Why is Mr. Axby unable to find a place to park? _____

10. What does he do when there is no place to park? _____

11. How often do the Axbys visit the cemetery? _____

12. What is the reason for their visits? _____

IX.   Commentary on Model

A.   1. Describe the street on which the Axbys live.

2. Discuss the result of Mrs. Axby's illness.

3. Describe the children and their activities.

4. Give an appropriate title to your composition.

B.   1. Discuss the points in the MODEL COMPOSITION that you like best.

2. Discuss the points in the MODEL COMPOSITION with which you disagree.

3. Explain paragraphs 1 and 2.

4. Give an appropriate title to your composition.

X.   Composition

A. Using the key words and sentences from the MODEL COMPOSITION, write your own composition on a related topic.

the street on which we live	at the same time
there are many trees	he loves to study
after a long illness	he is unable to learn well
he is the oldest	she is doing some chores
she was ill	her father bought a dress
she vacuums the room	a place to park
on rainy days	they remember the good times
once a year	cherish their memories
she was happy	

B. 1. Rewrite paragraph 2 of the MODEL COMPOSITION in the **I** person. Make all appropriate changes.

Example: **I** was ill during last week, etc.

2. Rewrite paragraph 3 in the **past tense**. Make all appropriate changes.

Example: Mr. Axby often **waited** in his car . . . .

C. Describe what you see in the picture below.

PART TWO

Writing the
Paragraph

Chapter Six

Outlining

Words to Remember:

OUTLINE = *related items, ideas*

ORGANIZATION and ANALYSIS

TOPIC OUTLINE = *short phrases, single words*

TOPIC SENTENCE = MAIN IDEA

I. *Model Composition*

A.   Winter Rain: A Fable

Even the hardest task is easier to accomplish with faith. A story I once heard will prove the point.

1. Once upon a time there lived a humble basket-weaver in a small town. He worked hard from dawn to dusk. His rewards were small. He had a wife and four children. Whenever he'd pity himself, he'd repeat the same old saying: "It seems like the poor must carry the burden of this world on their shoulders. The rich have fewer worries and less children to feed."

2. Listening to her husband's bitter complaints, the wife admonished him; "Quit your complaining and get on with your work. Keep the faith, and things will get better. Complaining never got things done."

3. The man was ashamed of having so little faith in himself. He turned his attention to the baskets waiting to be weaved and delivered. His wife and their oldest son helped with the work. Sometimes the man even whistled while he weaved the many baskets.

4. Winter arrived, and life came to a halt in the small town. All roads were covered with snow, and there was no way the baskets could be delivered to the market in the city. "If we could only manage till early spring, we'd be fine," the basket-weaver told his wife. "Keep the faith, believe, and things will happen," she repeated, as she went on with her work.

5. Their food supplies were almost gone, and the snow still covered the roads. There was no indication of a change in the weather. The basket-weaver worried silently because he was ashamed to complain to his smiling wife. She, too, was worried inwardly, but she knew that to complain would only worsen the situation.

6. The family got up early one morning, as usual. They were about to con-sume their last supply of food for breakfast. Suddenly, thunder was heard, and large drops of rain came falling. Everyone was so excited, they could not finish their breakfast. In the middle of winter rain fell! They ran outside and they drenched themselves in the falling rain. The roads would now be cleared. They could now travel to the city to deliver the merchandise! Everyone laughed and cried with joy. The woman clasped her husband's hand in her own. "Keep the faith," she said quietly. He understood.

B. **Composition by Degrees**

1. a. Copy the title of the MODEL COMPOSITION. _____
_____

   b. Copy the sentence that tells about the topic of the composition. __
_____

   c. Copy the phrase that tells about the man's vocation. _____
_____

   d. Copy the sentence that tells how much the man worked. _____
_____

   e. Copy the man's "complaint." _____
_____

2. a. Copy the sentence that tells why the wife admonished the basket-
weaver. _____
_____

   b. Copy the phrase that expresses the idea related to the title of the
composition. _____
_____

3. a. Copy the sentence that tells why the man was ashamed. _____
_____

   b. Copy the phrase that tells how the man behaved during work. _____
_____

4. a. Copy the phrase that tells why "life came to a halt." _____
_____

   b. Copy the phrase that tells what covered the roads. _____
_____

   c. Copy the phrase that tells how "things will happen." _____
_____

5. a. Copy the sentence that tells what "was almost gone." _____
_____

   b. Copy the phrase that tells what "covered the roads." _____
_____

   c. Copy the sentence that tells why the basket-weaver "worried
silently." _____
_____

   d. Copy the phrase that tells how the basket-weaver's wife worried. __
_____

6. a. Copy the phrase that tells when the family got up. _____

   _____

   b. Copy the sentence that tells what the family was about to do. _____

   _____

   c. Copy the phrase that tells what "was heard." _____

   _____

   d. Copy the phrase that tells what happened after the "thunder was heard." _____

   _____

   e. Copy the phrase that tells why everyone was excited. _____

   _____

   f. Copy the phrase that tells why the family was excited about the rain. _____

   _____

   g. Copy the expression that concludes the story on the beginning theme. _____

   _____

II.   Words in Context

A.   From the list of words and phrases preceding each section fill in each blank space provided in the text. You may use a selection more than once. Also, you may use more than one word in one blank space.

1. worked	dawn	lived	dusk	small
repeat	saying	seems	carry	pity
must	shoulders	have	less	feed

Once upon a time there _____ a humble basket-weaver in a _____ town. He _____ hard from _____ to _____ . Whenever he'd _____ himself, he'd _____ the same old _____ . "_____ like the poor _____ the burden of this world on their _____ . The rich _____fewer worries and children to _____ ."

2. bitter	quit	work	listening
get on	keep	things	admonished

_____ to her husband's _____ complaints, the wife _____ him; "_____your complaining and _____ with your_____ . _____ the faith, and _____ will get better."

3. turned	weaved	ashamed	waiting
faith	whistled	baskets	

The man was _____ of having so little _____ in himself. He _____
his attention to the baskets _____ to be _____ and delivered. It go so, the
man even _____ while he _____ the many _____ .

4. way	delivered	city	manage
halt	covered	only	arrived
spring			

Winter _____ and life came to a _____ in the small town. All
roads were _____ with snow, and there was no _____ the baskets could be
_____ to the market in the _____ . "If we could _____ till early _____
we'd be fine." He said.

5. almost	indication	silently	roads
weather	ashamed	worried	supplies

Their food _____ were _____ gone, snow still covered the _____ ,
and there was no _____ of a change in the _____ . The basket-weaver worried _____ because he was _____ to complain. His wife, too, was
_____ inwardly.

6. usual	food	thunder	got up	finish
middle	excited	rain	consume	laughed
cleared	travel	cried	woman	keep

The family _____ early one morning, as _____ . They were
about to _____ their last supply of _____ for breakfast. Suddenly, _____
was heard. In the _____ of winter _____ fell! Everyone was so
_____ , they could not _____ their breakfast. The roads would now
be _____ . They could now _____ to the city! They _____
and _____ with joy. The _____ clasped her husband's hand in
her own. " _____ the faith," she said silently. He understood.

B. Make the necessary change(s) when you substitute the new element into
your sentence.

> Example: Even the hardest **task** is easier to accomplish with faith.
> (tasks)
> Even the hardest tasks are easier to accomplish with faith.

1. a. **He** worked hard from dawn to dusk. (we)

   _____

   b. **His** rewards were small. (our)

   _____

   c. **He** had a wife and four children. (I)

   _____

   d. **The rich** have fewer worries. (they)

   _____

2. a. She was listening to her husband's **bitter complaints**. (stories)

   _____

   b. **His** wife admonished **him**. (my)

   _____

   c. **Things** will get better. (life)

   _____

3. a. **The man was** ashamed. (we)

   _____

   b. He turned his attention to the **baskets**. (work)

   _____

   c. **His wife and their oldest son** helped with the work. (they)

   _____

   d. **The man** whistled while **he** weaved. (I)

   _____

4. a. Winter arrived, and life came to a halt **in the small town**. (there)

   _____

   b. All **roads** were covered with snow. (streets)

   _____

   c. There was no way to deliver the **baskets**. (merchandise)

   _____

   d. **You** must believe, and things will happen. (we)

   _____

5. a. **Their** food supplies were almost gone. (our)

   _____

   b. **The basket-weaver** worried silently. (he)

   _____

   c. **He** was ashamed to complain to **his wife**. (I, her)

   _____

6. a. **The family** got up early one morning. (they)

_____

   b. **They** were about to consume **their** last food. (we)

_____

   c. **Everyone was** excited because of the rain. (they)

_____

   d. **They** could not finish **their** breakfast. (we)

_____

   e. **They** could now travel to the city. (she)

_____

   f. **They** cried with joy. (I)

_____

   g. "Keep the faith." **She** said quietly. **He** understood. (He, I)

_____

III. *Structures (Key words [phrases] for composition)*

A. Use the following key words [phrases] to form complete sentences. You may consult the MODEL COMPOSITION.

> Example: the task / is / with faith
> The hardest task is easier to accomplish with faith.

1. a. once / lived / basket-weaver _____

_____

   b. rewards / were _____

_____

   c. had / wife / children _____

_____

   d. poor / carry / burden / shoulders _____

_____

   e. rich / have / worries / children _____

_____

2. a. listening / husband's / complaints / the wife _____

_____

   b. quit / complaining / get on / work _____

_____

c. keep / faith _____

_____

d. things / get / better _____

_____

3. a. man / ashamed / little / faith / himself _____

_____

b. turned / attention / baskets / weaved / delivered _____

_____

c. wife / son / helped / work _____

_____

d. man / whistled / weaved / baskets _____

_____

4. a. life / came / halt / town _____

_____

b. roads / covered / snow _____

_____

c. no way / baskets / delivered _____

_____

d. manage / early / spring / we'd / fine _____

_____

e. she / went on / work _____

_____

5. a. supplies / gone / still / covered / roads _____

_____

b. indication / change / weather _____

_____

c. basket-weaver / worried _____

_____

d. she / complain / worsen / situation _____

_____

6. a. family / got up / morning _____

_____

b. they / about / consume / food / breakfast _____

_____

c. thunder / was heard / drops / came falling _____

_____

d. middle / winter / rain / fell _____

_____

e. everyone / was / excited / finish / breakfast _____

_____

f. they / ran / drenched / falling / rain _____

_____

g. roads / would / be cleared _____

_____

h. they / cried / joy _____

_____

i. woman / clasped / hand / own _____

_____

B. Supply the missing preposition for each blank space. You may consult the MODEL COMPOSITION.

Example: The woman clasped her husband's hand (in) her own.

1. a. A humble basket-weaver lived _____ a small town.

    b. He worked hard _____ dawn _____ dusk.

    c. The poor must carry the burden _____ this world _____ their shoulders.

    d. The rich have less children _____ feed.

2. a. Listening _____ her husband's complaints, the wife admonished him.

    b. Get _____ with your work.

3. a. He was ashamed _____ having little faith _____ himself.

    b. He turned his attention _____ the baskets.

    c. His wife and oldest son helped _____ the work.

4. a. Life came _____ a halt _____ the small town.

    b. Roads were covered _____ snow.

    c. Baskets could not be delivered _____ the market _____ the city.

5. a. There was no indication _____ a change _____ the weather.

    b. He was ashamed to complain _____ his wife.

6. a. They were about to consume their last supply _____ food _____ breakfast.

    b. Large drops _____ rain fell.

    c. _____ the middle _____ winter rain fell!

    d. They drenched themselves _____ the falling rain.

  e. They could now travel _____ the city.

  f. They laughed and cried _____ joy.

IV. *Grammar and Syntax [Points of Interest]*

Outlining is a necessary skill. It is useful in learning to read and write. An **outline** helps to understand the full meaning of written material.

A. Form and Structure (What is an outline?)

An **outline** is prepared as a plan and structure of any kind of writing. It is basically a listing of ideas and important points. Items that are of similar or related nature are grouped together. In this way, it is possible to show clearly and simply the relationship of things in one group, and to distinguish group I from group II. For example, we can organize the names of various books into three groups:

  I. FICTION
   A. *Gone with the Wind*
   B. *All Lie in Wait*
   C. *The Winds of War*

  II. BIOGRAPHY
   A. *Memoirs*
   B. *Diaries and Letters*
   C. *The War Years*

  III. DRAMA
   A. *The Death of a Salesman*
   B. *Romeo and Juliet*
   C. *Oedipus Rex*

The above **outline** is called **topic outline**. All of the objects listed here are related to each other; they are books. The **outline** classified and organized the books according to I. **Fiction**, II. **Biography** and III. **Drama**. The **topic outline** is composed of short **phrases** or **single** words. Generally these phrases or words are numbered (I., II., III., etc.) or lettered (A., B., C., etc.) to show a certain order and relation of ideas as shown above.

[NOTE: There are basically three types of outlines: the **topic outline**, the **paragraph outline** and the **sentence outline**. They are related in their use, however. The **topic outline** is of major concern here, since it governs the order of **composition**.]

B.   The Topic Sentence

The **topic sentence** expresses the **main idea** of a paragraph. It summarizes the whole paragraph, or tells the reader what the paragraph is about. The topic sentence is usually the first sentence of a paragraph. Some of the sentences that follow the topic sentence give it support. Other sentences in the paragraph expand the ideas expressed by the topic sentence and its supporting sentences.

> Example: **Even the hardest task is easier to accomplish with faith.** Once upon a time there lived a humble basket-weaver in a small town. He worked hard, and his rewards were small. He often complained about his fate to his wife. But his wife was cheerful. She encouraged the man to believe in himself. With faith things would be more easily done.

C.   Exercises

1. *Outlining*—Arrange the following lists of items into outlines that could be used in writing a theme.

a. A theme about **well-known people.** Organize the following list of names according to two groups:

> I. Male
> II. Female

Alexander the Great, John Adams, Sarah F. Adams, Maxwell Anderson, Ethel Barrymore, Dante Alighieri, Francis Bacon, Lady Ann Bacon, James Balfour, Honore de Balzac, Charles Beaudelaire, Bernard Baruch, Charlotte A. Barnard, Samuel Beckett, Ethel L. Beers, Ludwig van Beethoven, Isabella M. Beeton, Alexander Graham Bell, Stella Benson, Cyrano de Bergerac, Leon Blum, Humphrey Bogart, Simon Bolivar, Louis D. Brandeis, Charlotte Bronte, Martin L. King, Emily Bronte, Robert Browning, Elizabeth B. Browning, Albert Camus, Miguel de Cervantes, Paul Cezanne, Agatha Christie, Confucius, Joseph Conrad, David Crockett, Harry S. Truman, Pearl S. Buck, Thomas A. Edison, Margaret Fuller, Cornelia O. Skinner, Carl Sandburg, Elizabeth Wordsworth

b. A theme about **food.** Organize the following items according to five groups:

> I. Meats, fish, poultry, eggs

    II. Breads and cereals
   III. Dairy products
   IV. Fruits and vegetables
    V. Extras (sweets and desserts)

pork, wheat, bread, apple, potato, tomato, candy, sugar, salt, apricot, flounder, barley, beef, chocolate, pear, hot dog, cookies, rice, green beans, cherries, oatmeal, biscuit, cheese, milk, hamburger, bacon, creampuff, turkey, okra, eggplant, lobster, eggs, orange, veal, banana, corn, strawberry, beans, peas, chicken, squash, shrimp, ice cream, donuts, tuna, lollipop, dove, cake, pancake

2. *Topic sentence*—Identify the topic sentence (main idea) in each of the following paragraphs.

a. There are many ways in which our thinking is stimulated. To be productive individuals, we must think. When we study English, we think. We speak and create new thoughts. We write and think only in English. Thinking in one language, but learning another, makes it harder to progress creatively. When we study English, we must think in English.

b. The cosmopolitan nature of the English language is both an advantage and a disadvantage. On the one hand, its advantage is that it has drawn words from many sources. Also, each word comes with a precise definition. On the other hand, its disadvantage lies in the fact that these words are often very nearly alike in definition. To summarize, a writer not intimately familiar with their exact meanings will use them contrary to their correct usage.

c. It is important to use the right word in a given place. Therefore, the correct definition of a term must be ascertained lest one may regret having misused a word. For example, poor spelling is frequently the cause for misuse of words. Finally, unable to spell the effective word correctly, we will use a poor compromise, or an altogether wrong expression.

d. Advertising is an American way of life. Thus, Americans like advertising. Besides, people depend on advertisement in their daily life because they are consumers. The advertisers are manufacturers. Moreover, some advertisers are salesmen. Their merchandise needs advertising. Thus, every product is advertised. Most merchants buy ads for their products. In short, good advertising means success; bad advertising can mean failure.

V.   Idea Recognition

Copy from the MODEL COMPOSITION the sentences expressing:

A.   what is easier accomplished with faith . . .

_____

B.   who lived in a small town . . .

_____

C.   why the basket-weaver repeated the old saying . . .

_____

D.   what the poor must carry on their shoulders . . .

_____

E.   what the rich have less of . . .

_____

F.   why the wife admonished the basket-weaver . . .

_____

G.   why the man was ashamed . . .

_____

H.   why life came to a halt in the small town . . .

_____

I.   why there was no way to deliver the baskets to the city . . .

_____

J.   why the basket-weaver worried silently . . .

_____

K.   what would worsen the situation . . .

_____

L.   what followed the thunder . . .

_____

M.   why everyone was excited . . .

_____

N.   whose hand the woman clasped in her own . . .

_____

O.   what the basket-weaver understood . . .

_____

VI.   *Vocabulary Enrichment*

A.   Paraphrasing

The following are **paraphrases** (rephrasing expressions or words without changing their meaning) of expressions or words found in the narrative. Write the expressions found in the MODEL COMPOSITION that correspond to the paraphrases below.

> Example. a task to accomplish **a thing to do**

1. a person who weaves baskets _____
2. worked from early morning till late at night _____
3. got little for his work _____
4. is responsible for _____
5. told him to stop complaining _____
6. he felt sorry about his behavior _____
7. everything stopped _____
8. unable to take to town _____
9. don't lose hope _____
10. was worried secretly _____

B.   Lexical Units

Select the word (or phrase) from the following list that best completes each of the sentences below. You may use one selection more than once.

> Example: The hardest task is easier to **accomplish with faith.**
> The most difficult task is more easily **done when you believe in yourself.**

all day long	little pay	poor	nothing to eat
clear	pity	turned	unhappy
deliver	show		

1. He worked hard **from dawn to dusk.** _____he spent working.
2. His rewards were **small.** He received _____ for his work.
3. The basket-weaver was **poor.** That's why he'd _____ himself.
4. The rich have **fewer worries.** The_____people think so.
5. The husband **complained** bitterly. He was very _____ .
6. He was ashamed of his **lack of faith.** He _____ his attention to his work.
7. The roads were **covered with snow.** There was no way to _____ the baskets.
8. Their food supplies were **almost gone.** They would have _____ .

9. She worried **inwardly**, because she didn't want to _____ her concern to her family.

10. They **drenched** themselves in **the rain**. They were happy because the rain would _____ the roads.

C.   Related Words

Use related words to rewrite the following sentences without changing their meanings. Change the underlined word. Make further changes if necessary.

> Example: accomplished (v.)   accomplishment (n.)
> Even the hardest task is easier to **accomplish** with faith.
> Even the hardest task becomes an easier **accomplishment** with faith.

to work (v.)	to pity (v.)	to burden (v.)	to help (v.)
work (n.)	pity (n.)	burden (n.)	help (n.)
working (v.)		burdened (adj.)	helping (v.)

to admonish (v.)	to whistle (v.)	to carry (v.)
admonishment (n.)	whistle (n.)	carrying (v.)
admonishing (v.)	whistling (v.)	

1. He **worked** hard. _____

_____

2. The man **pitied** himself. _____

_____

3. The poor **carry** the **burden** of the world. _____

_____

4. The wife **admonished** the basket-weaver. _____

_____

5. His son and his wife **helped** with the work. _____

_____

6. The man **whistled while he worked.** _____

_____

VII.   Steps in Writing

A.   Add new words and revise the sentence, if necessary, to suit the changes indicated in parentheses.

Example: Even **the** hardest task is easier to accomplish with faith. (a)
Even **a hard** task is easier to accomplish with faith.

1. There lived **a humble** basket-**weaver** in a town. (many)

_____

2. **He** worked hard **from dawn to dusk**. (they, all day)

_____

3. **His** rewards were small. (their)

_____

4. **He'd** pity **himself**, and **he'd** repeat the saying. (I)

_____

5. **The poor** must carry the burden of this world. (we)

_____

6. **The rich have** fewer worries. (she)

_____

7. The wife admonished **him**. (her husband)

_____

8. Keep **the faith**. (believing in yourself)

_____

9. Complaining never got **things** done. (anything)

_____

10. **The man was** ashamed. (we)

_____

11. **He** turned **his** attention to the weaving. (I)

_____

12. **His wife and his son** helped him. (the others)

_____

13. **The man** whistled while he weaved. (they)

_____

14. **All roads were** covered with snow. (the road)

_____

15. **Their** food supplies were almost gone. (My)

_____

16. **The basket-weaver** worried silently. (I)

_____

17. **The family** got up early one **morning**. (we, day)

_____

18. **Everyone was** excited. (we)

_____

19. **The roads** would now be cleared. (it)

_____

20. **Everyone** laughed and cried with joy. (we)

_____

B.   Opposites

Use the **opposites** to rewrite the following sentences. Make the necessary changes to suit the new sentences. You may use a word more than once.

      Example: easier—harder
           Things are **easier** to accomplish with faith.
           Things are **harder** to accomplish without faith.

better	fewer	hard	humble	inwardly	little
oldest	big	small	worsen	quietly	

1. There lived a **haughty** basket-weaver in a small town. _____

_____

2. His work was very **light**. _____

_____

3. His rewards were **big**. _____

_____

4. The rich have **more** worries. _____

_____

5. Keep the faith, and things will get **worse**. _____

_____

6. The man was ashamed of having so **much** faith. _____

_____

7. The **youngest** son helped with the work._____

_____

8. Life came to a halt in the **small** town. _____

_____

9. The man worried **outwardly**. _____

_____

10. To complain would **better** the situation._____

_____

11. "Keep the faith," she said **loudly.** _____

_____

VIII.   *Comprehension*

A.   Complete the sentence and add as many related sentences as you can find in the MODEL COMPOSITION.

    Example: Even the hardest task **is easier to accomplish with faith.**

    1. Once upon a time _____

_____

    2. He worked hard _____

_____

    3. Whenever he'd pity himself _____

_____

    4. Listening to her husband's bitter complaints, _____

_____

    5. The man was ashamed _____

_____

    6. Winter arrived, _____

_____

    7. Their food supplies were almost gone, _____

_____

    8. The family got up early one morning, _____

_____

    9. Suddenly, thunder was heard, _____

_____

    10. Everyone laughed and cried _____

_____

B.   Answer each question with a complete sentence.

    Example: What kind of a task is easier to accomplish with faith?
            Even the hardest task is easier to accomplish with faith.

    1. Who lived in a small town? _____

_____

2. How did the basket-weaver work? _____

_____

3. What were his rewards? _____

_____

4. How many children did the basket-weaver have? _____

_____

5. When the weaver complained, what did his wife say to him? _____

_____

6. Does complaining get things done? _____

_____

7. What was the man ashamed of?_____

_____

8. Who helped the weaver with his work?_____

_____

9. What happened when winter arrived?_____

_____

10. What happened to the roads in the winter? _____

_____

11. When would the roads be cleared?_____

_____

12. Why did the basket-weaver worry? _____

_____

13. What was he ashamed to do? _____

_____

14. When did the family get up as usual? _____

_____

15. What was suddenly heard? _____

_____

16. Were the rain drops large? _____

_____

17. What was unusual about the rain? _____

_____

18. What would the rain do to the roads? _____

_____

19. How did this help the basket-weaver? _____

_____

20. What did the man understand at the end? _____
_____

IX.   *Commentary on Model*

A.   1. Describe the work of the basket-weaver.

2. Tell why the basket-weaver was discouraged.

3. Tell how his wife behaved.

4. Tell why the story is called "A Fable."

5. Give an appropriate title to your composition.

B.   1. Do you agree with the basket-weaver?

2. Do you agree with the basket-weaver's wife?

3. Tell why you agree or disagree?

4. Give an appropriate title to your composition.

X.   *Composition*

A.   Using the key words below and phrases from the MODEL COMPOSITION, write your own composition on a related topic. Organize an **outline**. Start the theme with a **topic sentence**.

once upon a time	he worked hard
small rewards	the poor carry burden
the rich have fewer worries	

B.   1. Rewrite section 1 of the MODEL COMPOSITION in the **we** person. Make all appropriate changes.

Example: Once upon a time **we** lived in a small town.

2. Rewrite section 5 in the **I** person. Make all appropriate changes.

Example: **My** food supplies were almost gone . . .

C.   Make an **outline** for the following themes:

1. how to prepare for a picnic

2. how to celebrate New Year's Eve

3. how to go about getting a job

4. how to organize a rescue operation at sea

D.   Write one **paragraph** about the picture below. Remember to include a **topic sentence**.

Chapter Seven

Elements of the Paragraph

Words to Remember:

Paragraph = *Topic Sentence*
Body
Conclusion (Transition)

Coherence

Topic Sentence = *Main Idea*
Body = *Development of Ideas*
Concluding Sentence = *End of Paragraph*

Transitional Phrases

consequently, therefore, likewise, however, yet, still,
moreover, furthermore, also, too,
first, besides, for example, as an illustration,
in conclusion, to conclude, in short, finally

I. Model Composition

A. The Town Fool: A Fable

The person who finds inner peace will discover happiness.

1. Everyone made fun of Clarence "the beggar." No one in town knew where he came from, consequently everyone was suspicious of this stranger. He simply appeared in town one day, and he stayed. Children ran after the haggard-looking man, mocking him both on and off the street. Likewise, some grown-ups jeered at him with contempt. However, there were others who permitted Clarence to earn a few coins by doing errands or manual work. In short, the town was learning to accept the beggar's presence as best it could.

2. The beggar's obvious contentment puzzled and annoyed almost everyone. Curious people regarded him as a kind of phenomenon. Therefore, they addressed the beggar in a sly way, trying to penetrate the shield of his contentment. Some of the people became angry at Clarence because he disregarded their attempts. It was all to no avail; Clarence kept his composure and also his friendly grin.

3. As time passed, the townspeople gradually became accustomed to the beggar's presence. They regarded him, therefore, with less curiosity. Many believed him to be unable to speak or to hear. "He's deaf and dumb," they said with a shrug, and they let the beggar be. Only the children still followed Clarence through the streets, although now with more amusement than hostility.

4. One day, the unexpected happened. It was going to be a day everyone would remember as long as they lived. The townspeople gathered in the market place. They were unhappy about the way the town was run by the Town Council. Likewise, they were not contented with themselves. They expressed their unhappiness in many different ways. Some shouted abuses. Others displayed posters with various slogans. Still others threatened with violence. Funny thing, there was not one voice heard in the defense of the Town Council.

5. Suddenly, the crowd grew silent. There were a few whispers heard here and there. "The fool, what does he want here?" "He ought to be run out of town!" "How dare he come here like this?" The cause of those remarks was Clarence "the beggar" who appeared at the scene with a large poster displaying only two sentences; MAN'S GREATEST LOSS IS THE LOSS OF HIS INNER PEACE! WHEN HARMONY PREVAILS WITHIN YOU, HAPPINESS COMES YOUR WAY. The words were printed in large letters with black paint on white cardboard. Clarence did not say one word, yet he spoke louder than all the shouting and threatening of the mob.

6. To make a long story short, it has been many years, and many generations have come and gone since those memorable events. Yet the townspeople speak about Clarence to this very day. They remember the lesson of inner peace and happiness as expressed by a humble beggar. No one remembers Clarence as the "town fool." His name is among the most respected names of the town.

B.   Composition by Degrees

1. a. Copy the title of the MODEL COMPOSITION. _____
   _____

   b. Copy the sentence that tells about the topic of the story. _____
   _____

   c. Copy the sentence that tells about the main character. _____
   _____

   d. Copy the sentence that tells about Clarence's appearance in town.__
   _____

   e. Copy the sentence that tells about the behavior of the children. ___
   _____

   f. Copy the sentence that tells how Clarence earned some money. ___
   _____

2. a. Copy the phrase that tells why the people were puzzled. _____
   _____

   b. Copy the phrase that tells what some people did to penetrate the shield of Clarence's contentment. _____
   _____

   c. Copy the sentence that tells why some people became angry at Clarence. _____
   _____

3. a. Copy the sentence that tells what happened in time. _____
   _____

   b. Copy the phrase that tells how the people regarded Clarence in time.
   _____

   c. Copy the sentence that tells who still followed the beggar. _____
   _____

4. a. Copy the sentence that tells what kind of a day it would be. _____
   _____

   b. Copy the sentence that tells why the townspeople gathered. _____
   _____

c. Copy the phrase that tells what some people shouted. ____

____

d. Copy the phrase that tells what some people threatened with. ____

____

5. a. Copy the sentence that tells what suddenly happened. ____

____

b. Copy the sentence that tells who was the cause of the people's remarks. ____

____

c. Copy the sentence that tells what Clarence carried. ____

____

d. Copy the sentence that tells how to become happy. ____

____

6. a. Copy the sentence that tells how long it has been since the events took place in town. ____

____

b. Copy the sentence that tells what the people remember. ____

____

c. Copy the sentence that tells how Clarence is remembered. ____

____

II. Words in Context

A. From the list of words and phrases preceding each section fill in each blank space. You may use a selection more than once. Also, you may use more than one word in one blank space.

1.
simply	suspicious	consequently	made
stayed	ran	haggard	in short
learning	presence	could	knew

Everyone _____ fun of Clarence "the beggar." No one in town
_____ where he came from, _____ everyone was _____ of
this stranger. He _____ appeared in town, and he _____. Children
_____ after the _____ looking man. _____ _____ _____,
the town was _____ to accept the beggar's _____ as best it _____ .

2.
| sly | therefore | phenomenon | regarded |
| contentment | people | angry | penetrate |

composure   grin

Curious people _____ him as a kind of _____ . _____ ,
they addressed the beggar in a _____ way, trying to _____ the shield
of his _____ . Some of them became _____ at Clarence. Clarence
kept his _____ and also his friendly _____.

3. gradually   regarded   passed   presence
   therefore   believed   curiosity   through
   speak   still

As time _____ , the townspeople _____ became accustomed to
the beggar's _____ . They _____ him, _____ , with less _____ .
Many _____ him to be unable to _____ or to hear. Only the
children _____ followed Clarence _____ the streets.

4. likewise   shouted   still   violence
   unhappy   gathered   place   run
   unexpected   everyone   lived   contented

One day, the _____ happened. It was going to be a day _____
would remember as long as they _____ . The townspeople _____ in
the market _____ . They were _____ about the way the town was
_____ by the Town Council. _____ , they were not _____ with themselves. Some _____ abuses. _____ others threatened with violence.

5. whispers   loss   peace   grew
   harmony   happiness   within   there

Suddenly, the crowd _____ silent. There were a few _____
heard here and _____ . Man's greatest _____ is the _____ of his
inner _____ ! When _____ prevails _____ you, _____ comes your way.

6. memorable   remember   peace   very
   happiness   humble   yet   short
   generations   gone

To make a long story _____ , it has been many years and many
_____ have come and _____ since those _____ events. _____ the
townspeople speak about Clarence to this _____ day. They _____ the
lesson of inner _____ and _____ as expressed by a _____ beggar.

B.   Make the necessary change(s) when you substitute the new element into
your sentence.

Example: **The person** who finds inner peace will discover happiness. (he)
He who finds inner peace will discover happiness.

1. a. **Everyone** made fun of Clarence. (the children)

   _____

   b. **No one** knew where he came from. (nobody)

   _____

   c. Children ran after the **haggard-looking man.** (beggar)

   _____

   d. **The town was** learning to accept his presence. (we)

   _____

2. a. **Curious people** regarded him as a phenomenon. (they)

   _____

   b. **They** addressed Clarence in a sly way. (the people)

   _____

   c. Some of **the people** became angry at Clarence. (them)

   _____

   d. **Clarence** kept **his** composure. (I, my)

   _____

3. a. **The townspeople** became accustomed to Clarence. (we)

   _____

   b. **They** regarded him with less curiosity. (the neighbors)

   _____

   c. **Many** believed him to be deaf and dumb. (some)

   _____

4. a. It was going to be a day **everyone** would remember. (we)

   _____

   b. **The townspeople** gathered in the market place. (men, women, and children)

   _____

   c. They were unhappy about the way **the town was** run. (things)

   _____

   d. **They** were not contented with **themselves.** (we)

   _____

   e. **They** expressed **their** unhappiness in many ways. (she)

   _____

   f. **Some** shouted abuses. (many)

   _____

g. **Others** threatened with violence. (few)

_____

5. a. Suddenly, **the crowd** grew silent. (they)

_____

b. **He** ought to be run out of town. (she)

_____

c. How dare **he** come here like this? (we)

_____

d. **Man's** greatest loss is the loss of **his** inner peace. (our)

_____

e. **He** spoke louder than all the shouting. (it)

_____

6. a. **The townspeople** speak about Clarence to this day. (they)

_____

b. **They** remember the lesson of inner peace. (we)

_____

c. **No one** remembers Clarence as the "town fool." (nobody)

_____

d. His **name** is respected. (memory)

_____

III.   Structures (Key words [phrases] for composition)

A.   Use the following key words (phrases) to form complete sentences. You may consult the MODEL COMPOSITION.

Example: person / finds / inner peace / happiness
         The person who finds inner peace will discover happiness.

1. a. everyone / fun / Clarence _____

_____

b. in town / knew / came from _____

_____

c. everyone / suspicious / of stranger _____

_____

d. children / ran / haggard / man _____

_____

e. grown-ups / jeered / with contempt _____

f. others / permitted / to earn / coins _____

g. town / was learning / the beggar's / presence _____

2. a. contentment / puzzled / annoyed _____

b. people / regarded / phenomenon _____

c. they / addressed / beggar / sly / way _____

d. some / became / angry _____

e. kept / composure / grin _____

3. a. they / regarded / loss / curiosity _____

b. many / believed / unable / speak / hear _____

c. only / children / followed _____

4. a. one day / unexpected / happened _____

b. going to be / a day / remember _____

c. townspeople / gathered / market place _____

d. they / unhappy / the way / town / run _____

e. expressed / unhappiness / different ways _____

f. they / not contented / themselves _____

g. displayed / posters / various / slogans _____

h. others / threatened / violence _____

   i. not one / voice / heard / defense / Town Council _____
_____

5. a. suddenly / crowd / silent _____
_____

   b. there / few / whispers / heard _____
_____

   c. greatest / loss / inner / peace _____
_____

   d. harmony / happiness / comes _____
_____

6. a. has been / many / years / generations_____
_____

   b. remember / lesson / inner peace / happiness _____
_____

   c. no one / remembers / town fool _____
_____

   d. name / among / respected / names _____
_____

B.   Supply the missing preposition for each blank space. You may consult the
MODEL COMPOSITION'

   Example: Everyone made fun __(of)__ Clarence.

1. a. No one _____ town knew where he came _____ .
   b. Everyone was suspicious _____ this stranger.
   c. He simply appeared _____town one day.
   d. Children ran _____ the haggard-looking man.
   e. They mocked him both _____ and _____the street.
   f. Others permitted Clarence to earn a few coins _____ doing errands.

2. a. They tried to penetrate the shield _____ his contentment.
   b. Some _____ the people became angry _____Clarence.
   c. It was all _____ no avail.
3. a. The townspeople became accustomed _____the beggar.
   b. They regarded him _____less curiosity.
   c. Only the children followed him _____the streets.

d. They followed him _____ more amusement than hostility.

4. a. They were unhappy _____ the way the town was run _____ the Town Council.

   b. They were not contented _____ themselves.

   c. They expressed their unhappiness _____ many ways.

   d. Some displayed posters _____ slogans.

   e. Still others threatened _____ violence.

5. a. He ought to be run out _____ town.

   b. The cause _____ those remarks was Clarence.

   c. He appeared _____ the scene.

   d. Man's greatest loss is the loss _____ his inner peace.

   e. When harmony prevails _____ you, happiness comes your way.

   f. The words were printed _____ large letters _____ black paint _____ white cardboard.

6. a. The people speak _____ Clarence _____ this very day.

   b. They remember the lesson _____ inner peace and happiness as expressed _____ a humble beggar.

   c. His name is _____ the most respected names _____ the town.

IV.   Grammar and Syntax [Points of Interest]

A.   Basically, an outline for a paragraph consists of one **summary sentence**. This sentence expresses the **main idea** discussed in the paragraph.

1. *Introductory sentence*—The **summary sentence** becomes an introductory sentence (topic sentence) within the paragraph itself. It expresses the **main idea** and it tells the reader what the paragraph is about. However, it does not include all the ideas to be developed in the paragraph. The **introductory sentence** is usually placed **first** in the paragraph.

> Example: "During the last ten years of the 19th century much progress was made in the field of psychology."

The rest of the paragraph will list and explain what this progress was.

2. *Paragraph coherence*—Sentences in a paragraph should **interrelate**. This means that each sentence ought to follow naturally from the force of the preceding one. In this manner, sentences within the paragraph are connected logically

(chronologically) and the reader is able to follow the thought easily. The paragraph shows **coherence**.

The harmony of a paragraph is generally secured by arranging certain ideas in a logical order. To help in the logical transition between sentences, one can use the following key words to express

    a. RESULT: consequently, therefore, thus, etc.

    b. COMPARISON: likewise, however, yet, still, etc.

    c. ADDITIONALS: first, moreover, also, too, furthermore, besides, etc.

    d. EXAMPLES: for example, as an illustration, etc.

    e. CONCLUSION: in conclusion to summarize, to conclude, in short, finally, etc.

3. *Body*—A well-written paragraph has a clear **central idea** stated in the topic sentence and a **body** that **supports** and **develops** that central idea. To be effective, the body of the paragraph must contain enough information pertaining to the topic sentence. It ought to deal only with subject matter that is related to the topic sentence.

> Example: "To make a telephone call from a public booth, follow these steps. First, remove the receiver and listen for the dial tone. Then put a coin in the slot. In most cases it will be a dime. Some calls will require additional coins. After you have deposited the correct amount, dial the number you want. When the call is completed, place the receiver back on the hook."

In the above paragraph, the main or **central idea** is expressed in the **topic** sentence. "To make a telephone call from a public booth . . ." The sentences which follow this central idea, enlarge and explain the topic sentence. All of the details mentioned in this paragraph deal with the process of "making a telephone call."

4. *The concluding (transitional) sentence*—This type of sentence is usually at the **end** of the paragraph. The **transitional** sentence does one of two things; it either concludes the paragraph or it prepares the reader for the following paragraph.

> Example: ". . . When the call is completed, place the receiver back on the hook."

"However, if the call is not completed, etc., etc."

[NOTE: The paragraph that follows the transitional sentence introduces a new idea; the possibility that a call **might not be completed**. The first sentence of this paragraph picks up where the transitional sentence left off, allowing for a logical sequence of ideas between paragraphs (Chapter 8).]

B.   Exercises

1. Each of the following paragraphs has a **main idea**, a **body**, and a **concluding** sentence. Identify these essential parts in each paragraph.

a. Advertising is an American way of life. Thus, Americans like advertising. Besides, people depend on advertisement in their daily life because they are consumers. The advertisers are manufacturers. Moreover, some advertisers are salesmen. Their merchandise needs advertising. Thus, every product is advertised. Most merchants buy ads for their products. In short, good advertising means success; bad advertising can mean failure.

b. The cosmopolitan nature of the English language is both an advantage and a disadvantage. On the one hand, its advantage is that it has drawn words from many sources. Also, each word comes with a precise definition. On the other hand, its disadvantage lies in the fact that these words are often very nearly alike in definition. To summarize, a writer not intimately familiar with their exact meanings will use them contrary to their correct usage.

c. It is important to use the right word in a given place. Therefore, the correct definition of a term must be ascertained lest one may regret having misused a word. For example, poor spelling is frequently the cause for misuse of words. Finally, unable to spell the effective word correctly, we will use a poor compromise, or an altogether wrong expression.

2. Each of the following "paragraphs" is incomplete. They are sets of sentences that lack either a **topic** sentence, a **body** or a **concluding** sentence. Read the "paragraphs" carefully and tell which of the essential parts is missing. Write the name of this element in the space provided.

a. On the one hand, its advantage is that it has drawn words from many sources. Also, each word comes with a precise definition. On the other hand, its disadvantage lies in the fact that these words are often very nearly alike in definition. To summarize, a writer not intimately familiar with their exact meanings will use them contrary to their correct usage.
Part missing: ————————————————————————————

b. Advertising is an American way of life. Thus, Americans like advertising. Besides, people depend on advertisement in their daily life because they are consumers. The advertisers are manufacturers. Moreover, some advertisers are salesmen. Their merchandise needs advertising. Thus, every product is advertised. Most merchants buy ads for their products.
Part missing: ——————————————————————————

c. It is important to use the right word in a given place. Finally, unable to spell the effective word correctly, we will use a poor compromise, or an altogether wrong expression.
Part missing: ——————————————————————————

3. Go back to EXERCISE 2. Insert one of the elements given below into its proper paragraph. Rewrite the entire paragraph.

a. In short, good advertising means success; bad advertising can mean failure.

b. The cosmopolitan nature of the English language is both an advantage and a disadvantage.

c. Therefore, the correct definition of a term must be ascertained lest one may regret having misused a word. For example, poor spelling is frequently the cause for misuse of words.

V.   *Idea Recognition*

Copy from the MODEL COMPOSITION the sentences expressing:

A.   what no one knew . . .

——————————————————————————

B.   who was suspicious . . .

——————————————————————————

C.   where Clarence appeared . . .

——————————————————————————

D.   who ran after Clarence . . .

——————————————————————————

E.   what the children did . . .

——————————————————————————

F.   what some grown-ups did . . .

——————————————————————————

G. who permitted Clarence to earn a few coins . . .

_____

H. how Clarence earned a few coins . . .

_____

I. what the town was learning . . .

_____

J. what puzzled and annoyed almost everyone . . .

_____

K. how the people addressed the beggar . . .

_____

L. why some people became angry at Clarence . . .

_____

M. what Clarence kept . . .

_____

N. what the town became accustomed to . . .

_____

O. how the people regarded Clarence . . .

_____

P. what happened one day . . .

_____

Q. who gathered in the market place . . .

_____

R. who shouted slogans . . .

_____

S. who appeared suddenly . . .

_____

T. what Clarence displayed . . .

_____

U. what the poster said . . .

_____

V. how the words were printed . . .

_____

W. who speaks about Clarence . . .

_____

X. what lesson the people remember . . .

_____

Y. where Clarence's name is . . .

_____

VI. *Vocabulary Enrichment*

A. Paraphrasing

The following are **paraphrases** (rephrasing expressions or words without changing their meaning) of expressions or words found in the narrative. Write the expressions found in the MODEL COMPOSITION that correspond the paraphrases below.

Example: to find inner peace   **to become peaceful inwardly**

1. people laughed at him _____
2. they didn't trust _____
3. they were cruel _____
4. shouted angrily _____
5. went to fetch things _____
6. they considered him _____
7. he was peaceful and satisfied _____
8. he kept his calmness _____
9. a smile on his face _____
10. they were delighted _____
11. everyone came together _____
12. threw insults _____
13. showed up at the gathering _____
14. would be remembered _____

B. Lexical Units

Select the word (phrase) from the following list that best completes each of the sentences below. You may use one selection more than once.

Example: The person who finds **inner peace** will discover happiness.
Happy is the person who is **peaceful inwardly**.

| contentment | ignored | defend | accepted | suspicious |
| remained | find out | composure | angry | fool |

1. No one **knew where he came from**. Everyone was _____ .
2. He **came to town** one day. And he _____there.

3. Children **mocked** the beggar. But he did not _____ himself.

4. The people were **puzzled**. The source of their puzzlement was the beggar's _____ .

5. They addressed the beggar in a **sly way**. The people wanted to _____ about him.

6. Some people were **angry** at Clarence. But Clarence _____them.

7. Gradually the townspeople became **accustomed** to the beggar's presence. They _____ his being there.

8. People tried to **make him angry**. But Clarence kept his _____ .

9. The people **shouted abuses**. They were _____ .

10. People remember Clarence's **lesson of inner peace**. No one remembers him as a _____ .

C.   Related Words

Use related words to rewrite the following sentences without changing their meanings. Change the underlined word. Make further changes if necessary.

    Example: suspicious (adj.)   to suspect (v.)
            Everyone **was suspicious** of this stranger.
            Everyone **suspected** this stranger.

to appear (v.)	contemptuous (adj.)	to puzzle (v.)
appearance (n.)	contempt (n.)	puzzlement (n.)
curious (adj.)	to amuse (v.)	to be hostile (v.)
curiosity (n.)	amusement (n.)	hostility (n.)
angry (adj.)	to whisper (v.)	
anger (n.)	whisper (n.)	

1. He simply **appeared** in town. _____

_____

2. They regarded him with **contempt**. _____

_____

3. The beggar's contentment **puzzled** the people. _____

_____

4. Some became **angry** at Clarence. _____

_____

5. They regarded him with less **curiosity**. _____

_____

6. Children followed Clarence with more **amusement** than **hostility**. _____

7. There were a few **whispers**. _____

VII. Steps in Writing

A.   Add new words and revise the sentence to suit the changes indicated in parentheses.

> Example: The **person** who **finds** inner peace will discover happiness. (people)
> The **people** who **find** inner peace will discover happiness.

1. **Everyone was** suspicious of the beggar. (they)

2. **He** simply appeared in town. (I)

3. **Children** ran after the beggar. (she)

4. **Some grown-ups** jeered at him. (the townspeople)

5. There were **others** who gave Clarence work. (people)

6. The town was learning to accept **the beggar**. (Clarence)

7. **Curious people** regarded him as a kind of phenomenon. (we)

8. **They** addressed **the beggar** in a sly way. (she, him)

9. **Some people** became angry. (I)

10. **Clarence kept his** composure. (they)

11. **Many** believed him to be deaf. (he)

12. Only **the children** still followed Clarence. (we)

13. The **townspeople** gathered in the market place. (they)

_____

14. **They** expressed **their** unhappiness. (we, our)

_____

15. **Some** shouted abuses. (they)

_____

16. **The crowd** grew silent. (she)

_____

17. **Man's** greatest loss is the loss of **his** inner peace. (our)

_____

18. **Clarence** did not say one word. (I)

_____

19. **They** remember the lesson. (we)

_____

20. **His** name is among the most respected names. (Clarence's)

_____

B.   Opposites

Use the opposites to rewrite the following sentences. Make the necessary changes to suit the new sentences. You may use a word more than once.

> Example: peace—unrest   happiness—unhappiness
> He who finds **peace** will discover **happiness**.
> He who finds **unrest** will discover **unhappiness**.

disliked	dissatisfaction	indifferent	many
unexpected	gradually	friendly	reject
accused	loudly	most	silent
unhappy	sly		

1. Everyone **liked** Clarence. _____

_____

2. Others permitted the beggar to earn **a few** coins. _____

_____

3. The town was learning to **accept** Clarence. _____

_____

4. The beggar's **contentment** puzzled the people. _____

_____

5. **Curious** people regarded him as a phenomenon. _____

6. They addressed the beggar in **an open** way. _____

7. Clarence kept his **unfriendly** grin. _____

8. The people **suddenly** became accustomed to Clarence. _____

9. One day the **expected** happened. _____

10. The people were **happy** with the Town Council. _____

11. Everyone **defended** the Town Council. _____

12. Suddenly, the crowd grew **loud**. _____

13. Clarence's poster spoke **silently**. _____

14. His name is among the **least** respected names. _____

VIII.   Comprehension

A.   Complete the sentence and add as many related sentences as you can find in the MODEL COMPOSITION.

Example: The person who finds inner peace **will discover happiness.**

1. Everyone made fun of Clarence _____
_____
_____

2. No one knew where he came from, _____
_____
_____

3. Children ran after the haggard-looking man, _____
_____
_____

4. The beggar's contentment _____

5. Therefore, they addressed the beggar in a sly way _____

6. Some people became angry at Clarence _____

7. As time passed, _____

8. Only the children _____

9. One day, the unexpected happened. _____

10. The townspeople gathered in the market place. _____

11. They expressed their unhappiness in many different ways. _____

12. The crowd grew silent. _____

13. The cause of those remarks was Clarence _____

14. Clarence did not say one word, _____

15. To make a long story short, _____

B. Answer each question with a complete sentence.

Example: What will the person discover?
The person will discover happiness.

1. Who made fun of Clarence? _____
_____

2. Did the people know where he came from? _____
_____

3. What happened one day? _____
_____

4. Who jeered at Clarence? _____
_____

5. Who permitted him to earn a few coins? _____
_____

6. What was the town learning? _____
_____

7. What puzzled almost everyone? _____
_____

8. How did some people address the beggar? _____
_____

9. Why did they address him in a sly way? _____
_____

10. Why did some people become angry at Clarence? _____
_____

11. How did the townspeople regard "the beggar"? _____
_____

12. What did the people say about him? _____
_____

13. How did the children follow Clarence through the streets? ____
_____

14. What kind of a day was it going to be? _____
_____

15. Who gathered in the market place? Why? _____
_____

16. How did the people express their unhappiness? _____
_____

17. Did anyone come to the defense of the Town Council? ____
_____

18. Why did the crowd grow suddenly silent? _____
_____

19. What did Clarence carry? _____
_____

20. What did the poster say? _____

_____

21. Do the people still remember Clarence? _____

_____

22. What do they remember about Clarence? _____

_____

23. How is his name regarded in town? _____

_____

IX.   Commentary on Model

A.   Using the key words and phrases from the MODEL COMPOSITION, write your own composition consisting of two paragraphs on a related topic.

suspicious of stranger	mocking the man
errands or manual work	peace and happiness
keep composure	unhappy with self
harmony prevails	respected name

B.   1. Rewrite section 4 of the MODEL COMPOSITION in the **we** person. Make all appropriate changes.

Example: It was going to be a day **we** would remember . . .

2. Rewrite section 6 in the **she** person. Make all appropriate changes.

Example: Yet **she** speaks about Clarence . . .

C.   1. Write about the **lesson** you've learned from the "Fable."

2. Write about the points you agree with.

3. Write about the points you disagree with.

4. Give an appropriate title to your composition.

X.   Composition

A.   Select three topics below and write one paragraph on each. Remember to include an introductory (topic) sentence within the paragraph itself. Follow the **topic sentence** with a **body** and the **concluding** statement.

1. how to change a car tire

2. how to climb a mountain

3. how to say "good night" to a date

4. description of the person you love

5. description of a flower

B.   Write one **paragraph** about the picture below. Remember to include all paragraph elements.

PART THREE

Writing
the Composition

Chapter Eight

Development of Composition

I.   *Model Composition*

A.   World University Community: A Dream

1. All roads have one particular characteristic in common; they accommodate people of all nationalities, creeds and different physical and psychological features. All these people are constantly moving toward a goal that became dear to the heart of every striving individual: the road to a complete and lasting peace. Such peace, we believe, will be finally achieved by students of all nations uniting into a World University Community.

2. A Community composed of students of all nations throughout the world will be bound by one great goal: the proposition to maintain peace. The student is, after all, the life-giving substance for the world, as is the blood to the body. As the roads to peace become narrow and corroded through ignorance and misunderstanding among human beings, so do sick arteries delay the flow of blood.

3. The road to peace is filled with obstacles. These obstacles can be cleared with good will and enlightened action. The student of the world will realize that he is the future of all walks of life on earth: the statesman, the doctor, the lawmaker, the educator of tomorrow. A great responsibility rests on his shoulders, and he will be strong and faithful to the ideas expressed by the word: STUDENT.

4. Many travel to study in foreign countries. They come among strange people and new customs. Their reactions are varied. Yet, most students make a similar observation that people, wherever they may be, are identical in one aspect: they walk the road of life common to all mankind. Students have the opportunity to discuss and argue about various controversial issues. However, they soon find their place and walk side-by-side with others. They argue for the improvement of things rather than for their destruction.

5. The effect of the written and spoken argument has proven successful in the past. We remember the old saying: "The pen is mightier than the sword." Physical violence and brutality are replaced by the ability to walk the road to communication and understanding. We will repeat our attempts until the bonds of helplessness are torn and we are free to practice within the walls of the Universe that which was taught within the walls of the University. We take this road, although a winding and tiresome one, because just ahead of us lies our goal, the state of peace, love and understanding: WORLD UNIVERSITY COMMUNITY.

B.   **Composition by Degrees**

1. a. Copy the title of the MODEL COMPOSITION. ＿＿＿＿＿＿
   _____

   b. Copy the sentence that tells what "all roads have in common." ＿＿＿
   _____

   c. Copy the sentence that tells where "all people are constantly mov-
      ing." ＿＿＿＿＿＿＿＿＿＿＿＿＿＿＿＿＿＿＿＿＿＿＿
   _____

   d. Copy the sentence that tells how "peace can be achieved." ＿＿＿＿
   _____

2. a. Copy the sentence that tells what will "bind a student community."
   _____

   b. Copy the phrase that tells what kind of "substance" the student is.
   _____

   c. Copy the phrase that tells how the "roads to peace" become. ＿＿
   _____

   d. Copy the sentence that tells why the roads to peace become "nar-
      row." ＿＿＿＿＿＿＿＿＿＿＿＿＿＿＿＿＿＿＿＿＿＿＿
   _____

3. a. Copy the phrase that tells what "the road to peace is filled with."
   _____

   b. Copy the sentence that tells how the "obstacles and narrow pas-
      sages" can be cleared. ＿＿＿＿＿＿＿＿＿＿＿＿＿＿＿＿
   _____

   c. Copy the sentence that tells what the student "will realize." ＿＿＿
   _____

   d. Copy the phrase that tells what "rests on the student's shoulders." ＿
   _____

4. a. Copy the sentence that tells where "many travel." ＿＿＿＿＿＿
   _____

   b. Copy the sentence that tells what "observation" most students make.
   _____

   c. Copy the sentence that tells what the students "argue about." ＿＿
   _____

5. a. Copy the old saying. ＿＿＿＿＿＿＿＿＿＿＿＿＿＿＿＿
   _____

b. Copy the phrase that tells what replaces violence and brutality. _____

_____

c. Copy the sentence that tells what the student will practice "within the walls of the Universe." _____

_____

d. Copy the sentence that tells what "goal lies ahead." _____

_____

II.   *Words in Context*

A.   From the list of words preceding each section fill in each blank space. You may use a selection more than once. Also, you may use more than one word in one blank space.

1. nationalities   goal   common   particular
   constantly   dear   physical   features
   accommodate   complete   striving

All roads have one _____ characteristic in_____; they
_____ people of all_____, creeds and different _____and psychological
_____ . All these people are _____ moving toward a _____
that became _____to the heart of every _____ individual; the
road to a _____ and lasting peace.

2. great   composed   world
   proposition   maintain   nations

A Community _____of students of all_____throughout the
_____will be bound by one_____goal: the_____ to_____peace.

3. obstacles   cleared   filled   passages
   widened   enlightened   spark

The road to peace is _____with _____ , natural and man-made.
_____and narrow_____ in this road can be _____ and _____
with each added_____of good will and _____ action.

4. foreign   new   travel   among
   students   reactions   opportunity   discuss
   argue   issues

Many _____ to study in _____ countries. They come _____ strange people and _____ customs. Their _____ are varied. They have the _____ to _____ and _____ about various controversial _____ .

5.
written	remember	effect	proven
violence	ability	winding	brutality
pen	past	mightier	communication
peace	university	love	sword
ahead	understanding		

The _____ of the _____ and spoken argument has _____ successful in the _____ . We _____ the old saying: "The _____ is _____ than the _____ ." Physical _____ and _____ are replaced by the _____ to walk the road to _____ and _____ . We take this road, although a _____ and tiresome one, because just _____ lies our goal, the state of _____ , _____ , and _____ : WORLD _____ COMMUNITY.

B. Make the necessary change(s) when you substitute the new element into your sentence.

> Example: **All roads have** one particular characteristic in common. (every)
>
> **Every road has** one particular characteristic in common.

1. a. **They accommodate** people of all nationalities. (it)

   _____

   b. **All these people** are constantly moving toward a goal. (we)

   _____

   c. **Peace** will finally be achieved by students. (understanding)

   _____

2. a. **The student is** the life-giving substance for the world. (they)

   _____

   b. The **roads** to peace **become** narrow and corroded. (road)

   _____

3. a. **Obstacles** can be cleared. (they)

   _____

   b. The **student** of the world **is** the future of all life. (students)

   _____

    c. A great responsibility rests on **his** shoulders. (our)

_____

  4. a. **Many travel** to study in foreign countries. (she)

_____

    b. **They come** among strange people. (he)

_____

    c. **Their** reactions are varied. (our)

_____

    d. Most **students** make a similar observation. (of us)

_____

    e. **The students** have an opportunity to discuss many issues. (we)

_____

    f. **They** soon **find their** place. (she)

_____

    g. **They argue** for the improvement of things. (he)

_____

  5. a. The **effect** of the written and spoken argument **is** successful. (effects)

_____

    b. **Physical violence and brutality are** replaced by understanding. (it)

_____

    c. **We** will repeat **our** attempts. (she)

_____

    d. **We take** this road. (he)

_____

    e. Just ahead lies **our** goal. (their)

_____

III. Structures (Key words [phrases] for composition)

A. Use the following key words [phrases] to form complete sentences. You may consult the MODEL COMPOSITION.

      Example: roads / have / characteristic / common
           All roads have one particular characteristic in common.

  1. a. they / accommodate / nationalities _____

_____

    b. people / moving / goal _____

c. became / heart / striving / individual _____

d. road / complete / lasting / peace _____

e. peace / finally / by students / all nations _____

2. a. students / bound / proposition / maintain peace _____

b. student / is / substance / world _____

c. roads / peace / become / ignorance _____

d. arteries / delay / flow _____

3. a. road / peace / filled / obstacles _____

b. narrow passages / cleared / spark / good will _____

c. the student / realize / the future / on earth _____

d. responsibility / rests / on shoulders _____

e. will be / faithful / to ideals / expressed _____

4. a. many / travel / study / foreign country _____

b. they / come / strange people / new customs _____

c. their / reaction / varied _____

d. students / make / observation _____

e. people / are / identical _____

f. they / walk / road / common / all mankind _____

g. students / have / opportunity / discuss / issues _____

_____

h. they / find / place / walk / others _____

_____

5. a. effect / written / spoken / argument / proven / successful _____

_____

b. pen / mightier / sword _____

_____

c. violence / brutality / replaced / ability / communication _____

_____

d. we / repeat / attempts _____

_____

e. bonds / helplessness / torn _____

_____

f. we / are / free / practice / walls / Universe _____

_____

g. we / take / road _____

_____

h. just / ahead / lies / goal _____

_____

B. Supply the missing **preposition** for each blank space. You may consult the MODEL COMPOSITION.

Example: All roads have one characteristic ___(in)___ common.

1. a. They accommodate people _____ all nationalities.
   b. All these people are moving _____ a goal.
   c. It became dear_____ the heart of every individual.
   d. This is the road_____ a lasting peace.
   e. It will be achieved _____ students_____ all nations.

2. a. A Community is composed _____ students _____ all nations.
   b. This is the proposition _____maintain peace.
   c. The roads _____peace become narrow.

3. a. The road _____ peace is filled _____obstacles.
   b. The student is the future _____ all life_____ earth.
   c. A great responsibility rests _____ his shoulders.

  d. He must be strong and faithful _____ the ideals which are expressed _____ the word: STUDENT.

 4. a. Many travel _____ study _____foreign countries.

  b. They come_____ strange people and new customs.

  c. The students have the opportunity to talk _____various issues.

  d. They find their place side- _____ -side _____ others.

 5. a. The effect_____the written argument has proven successful.

  b. Violence and brutality are replaced _____the ability _____ walk the road _____communication and understanding.

  c. Just ahead _____us lies our goal.

IV. *Grammar and Syntax [Points of Interest]*

A. Types of Paragraphs

 1. *Introductory*—The first paragraph is especially important in a composition. It serves a double purpose: while it tells the reader about the **subject** to be discussed, the opening paragraph also makes him want to **read on**. Thus, the introductory paragraph is an **interest-catching** device. It serves the composition in the same way a topic sentence serves the paragraph: as a summary of the composition.

    Example: Thieves found out they were wrong when they thought they could make some money by stealing a car from the Madrid Motor Co.

 2. *Main*—Generally, the main paragraph of a composition further discusses the ideas introduced in the first paragraph. The main paragraph provides **support** for the general ideas expressed in the introduction; it is, therefore, related to the topic sentence. The main paragraph may be one of the longest of the composition; however, it is its **subject matter** that is most important, not its length. The main paragraph may also be considered the **body of a composition**.

    Example: Police disclosed Tuesday that none of the local car lots would buy the stolen car. And, Inspector Barry Salinas said, the thieves became so desperate they even tried to sell the car back to the Madrid Motor Co.

 3. *Concluding*—The concluding paragraph can do several things: it can **summarize** the preceding material; it may **introduce** a new point while it re-

states the old; it may be a quiet ending to a composition or it may be made exciting and full of suspense.

> Example: When the Madrid Motor Co. refused to purchase the car, Salinas said, the thieves took it to Highway Ridge where they dumped it over an embankment.

B.   Arrangement and Order of Paragraphs

1. *Interrelationship*—Just as it is important to maintain a clear order within the paragraph itself, so it is within a composition where one follows a definite interrelationship of paragraphs. An effort must be made, therefore, to clearly state a **central idea** that bears a definite **relationship** to preceding as well as following paragraphs.

2. *Transition*—Oftentimes, an entire paragraph will serve as a transition. A transitional paragraph comes at a point in a composition where the writer wants **to start** on a new idea because he has finished with the previous **main point**. Various transitional devices are used to connect paragraphs. In addition to the transitional phrases introduced in Chapter VII, one may also use such transitional devices as **pronouns**, which make reference to items used previously, or the **repetition** of the very **item already mentioned**.

C.   Coherence and Proportion

In order to present a coherent picture of a composition the paragraphs are linked together by some common devices: **key words** are repeated, **pronouns** are used in reference to preceding nouns, **transitional connectives** are used (Chapter Seven), and reference is made to a common subject, event, or a significant idea that appears in previous as well as in the succeeding paragraphs. By using such devices, a writer weaves paragraphs into a unified composition.

There is no rule governing the length of a paragraph. Generally, a paragraph consists of more than one sentence but should not exceed a full page.

> Example: Thieves found out they were wrong when they thought they could make some money by stealing a car from the Madrid Motor Co.
>
> Police disclosed Tuesday that none of the local car lots would buy the stolen car. And, Inspector Barry Salinas said, the thieves became so desperate they even tried to sell the car back to the Madrid Motor Co.
>
> When the Madrid Motor Co. refused to purchase the car, Salinas said, the thieves took it to Highway Ridge

where they dumped it over an embankment.

D. Exercises

1. The following paragraphs are part of a newspaper article dealing with one **main idea**: the rains came too late for the Midwest drought. Arrange the paragraphs **chronologically**, beginning with the **introductory**, followed by the **main** and **concluding** paragraphs.

The full effect of the drought, which some experts call the worst since the Dust Bowl days of the 1930s, has yet to come to light. But thus far it is clear that the drought will be felt around the world.

The long-awaited rains have fallen over the drought-parched midlands, rattling through the dried and yellowed leaves of what was to be a bumper corn crop but producing little more than mud on the heat-cracked farmland.

The great drought of 1974 appears to have ended with the rainfall, but consumers and farmers may have to live with its effects for years to come.

In many parts of the corn belt, the rains were too late to help the crops—in some cases the rain just made things tougher.

2. Arrange the paragraphs chronologically by placing the **introductory**, **main**, and **concluding** paragraphs in order. Give a **headline** title.

Police disclosed Tuesday that none of the local car lots would buy the stolen car. And, Inspector Barry Salinas said, the thieves became so desperate they even tried to sell the car back to the Madrid Motor Co.

Thieves found out that they were wrong when they thought they could make money by stealing a car from the Madrid Motor Co.

When the Madrid Motor Co. refused to purchase the car, Salinas said, the thieves took it to Highway Ridge where they dumped it over an embankment.

3. The following two newspaper articles lack either the **introductory** or **concluding** paragraphs. Select the missing paragraph from those given following the article. Rewrite the completed articles.

a. Pronounced dead at the scene was Shay Lessing, according to the Department of Public Safety investigators.

The mother, Mary Lessing, 20, of Castroville, was listed Monday in satisfactory condition at Methodist Hospital in San Antonio.

The DPS officers said the auto left the roadway and plunged down a bridge abutment to the bottom of a creek bed.

b. Reduced speed limits, triggered by the energy shortage, are getting more credit than they deserve for the reduction of highway deaths in the nation, according to the American Medical Association.

"We hope, of course, that the nationwide downward trend continues, but we believe that the savings in lives cannot honestly be attributed to any great extent to the reduction in the speed limit," Lee N. Hames, AMA director of safety education, said in an editorial in the current edition of the Journal of the American Medical Association.

While speed limits have been reduced to 55 miles per hour, Hames said that most traffic deaths occur at speeds under 55.

A two-year-old child was killed and the mother seriously injured in a one-car accident at 11 p.m. Sunday about one mile east of here on U.S. 90.

V. *Idea Recognition*

Copy from the MODEL COMPOSITION the sentences expressing:

A.   what characteristic all roads have . . .

_____

B.   toward what people constantly move . . .

_____

C.   what will finally be achieved . . .

_____

D.   by whom it will be achieved . . .

_____

E.   who will be bound by one goal . . .

_____

F.   what the proposition will be . . .

_____

G.   what the student is . . .

_____

H.   why the roads to peace become narrow . . .

_____

I.   how the roads compare to arteries . . .

_____

J. what the road to peace is filled with . . .

_____

K. what kind of obstacles they are . . .

_____

L. what can be cleared and widened . . .

_____

M. how the roads can be widened . . .

_____

N. what the student will realize . . .

_____

O. what rests on the student's shoulders . . .

_____

P. what the student will be faithful to . . .

_____

Q. who travels to foreign countries . . .

_____

R. what kind of observation most students make . . .

_____

S. what opportunities the students have . . .

_____

T. what they argue for . . .

_____

U. what has proven successful . . .

_____

V. what we remember . . .

_____

W. what is mightier than the sword . . .

_____

X. until when the students will repeat their attempts . . .

_____

Y. what lies just ahead . . .

_____

VI. *Vocabulary Enrichment*

A. **Paraphrasing**

The following are **paraphrases** (rephrasing expressions or words without changing their meaning) of expressions or words found in the narrative. Write the expressions found in the MODEL COMPOSITION that correspond to the paraphrases below.

>Example: have a particular characteristic
>**they are similar to one another**

1. make space available _____
2. they are in motion _____
3. become fond of _____
4. countries getting together _____
5. having one purpose _____
6. a desire for tranquility _____
7. peaceful attempts become harder _____
8. they don't allow the flow _____
9. there are many difficulties _____
10. he has to do it _____
11. spoken thoughts _____
12. behave differently _____
13. find out the same thing _____
14. talk about things they disagree on _____
15. they get "with it" _____
16. discuss how to make things better _____
17. go on trying _____

B. Lexical Units

Select the word (phrase) from the following list that best completes each of the sentences below. You may use a selection more than once.

>Example: All roads have one **particular characteristic** in common.
>They all **accommodate** many people.

committed	misunderstanding	approaching
ignorance	unite	good will
enlightened action	destruction	strong

1. People are constantly **moving toward** a goal. They are _____ it.
2. Peace can be achieved by **students of all nations**. The students will _____ .
3. The students will be **bound** by one goal. They will be_____to this goal.
4. The road to peace becomes **corroded** and **narrow**. There is no peace because of _____ and_____ .
5. The **obstacles** can be **cleared**. Understanding comes through _____ and _____ _____ .
6. The student has a great **responsibility**. He must be _____.
7. The students argue to **improve** things. They want to prevent _____ .

C. Related Words

Use related words to rewrite the following sentences without changing their meanings. Change the underlined word(s). Make further changes if necessary.

> Example: to move (v.)   moving (v.)
>   People are constantly **moving**.
>   People **move** constantly.

to strive (v.)	to last (v.)	to unite (v.)
striving (adj.)	lasting (adj.)	uniting (v.)
		united (adj.)

to propose (v.)	similar (adj.)	to discuss (v.)
proposing (v.)	similarly (adv.)	discussing (v.)
proposition (n.)		discussion (n.)

to improve (v.)	to observe (v.)
improvement (n.)	observation (n.)

1. The goal is dear to every **striving** individual. _____

2. This is the road to a **lasting** peace. _____

3. Students of all nations will **unite** into a World University Community.

4. This Community is composed of students who **propose** to maintain peace. _____

5. Most students make a **similar observation about** other people. _____

6. The students have an opportunity **to discuss** many issues. _____

7. They argue **for the improvement** of things. _____

VII. Steps in Writing

A.   Add new words and revise the sentence to suit the changes indicated in parentheses.

> Example: **All roads have** one particular characteristic in common. (every)
> **Every road has** one particular characteristic in common.

1. **They accommodate** people of all nationalities. (she)

2. **All these people** are moving toward a goal. (every man)

3. **Understanding** leads to complete peace. (it)

4. **The student is** the life-giving substance for the world. (students)

5. The **roads** to peace **become** narrow. (road)

6. **He is** the **statesman** of tomorrow. (they)

7. **Many travel** to study in foreign countries. (the student)

8. **Their** reactions are varied. (her)

9. **Most** students make a similar observation. (all)

10. **The students** have an opportunity to discuss many issues. (I)

11. **They** soon **find their** place. (we)

12. **They argue** for the improvement of things. (she)

_____

13. The **effect** of the written argument **has** proven effective. (effects)

_____

14. **We** will repeat **our** attempts. (I)

_____

15. **We are** free to practice what **we learn**. (he)

_____

16. **We take** this road. (she)

_____

17. Ahead of **us** lies **our** goal. (him)

_____

B. **Opposites**

Use the opposites to rewrite the following sentences. Make the necessary changes to suit the new sentences. You may use a word more than once.

> Example: particular—usual
>> All roads have one **particular** characteristic in common.
>> All roads have one **usual** characteristic in common.

successful	common	improvement	mightier	winding
faithful	lasting	delay	sick	long
strong	narrow	complete	natural	quickly
ignorance				

1. People have **different** physical features. _____

_____

2. All people are **slowly** moving forward. _____

_____

3. The road to a **partial** peace is **brief**. _____

_____

4. They want a **temporary** peace. _____

_____

5. The roads to peace become **wide** through **knowledge**. _____

_____

6. The arteries **quicken** the flow of **healthy** blood. _____

_____

7. There are **unnatural** obstacles. _____

_____

8. Man must be **weak** and **unfaithful.** _____

_____

9. They argue for the **destruction** of things. _____

_____

10. The written word has proven **unsuccessful.** _____

_____

11. The word is **weaker** than the sword. _____

_____

12. The road is **straight.** _____

_____

VIII. Comprehension

A.   Complete the sentence and add as many related sentences as you can find in the MODEL COMPOSITION.

> Example: All roads have one particular characteristic in common; **they accommodate people of all nationalities, creeds and different physical and psychological features, in their walks of life.**

1. All these people are constantly moving toward a goal _____

_____

_____

2. A community composed of students _____

_____

_____

3. The student is, _____

_____

_____

4. The roads to peace become narrow and corroded _____

_____

_____

5. The road to peace is filled with obstacles, _____

_____

_____

6. The student of the world will realize _____

_____

7. Many travel _____

8. Yet, most students make a similar observation _____

9. The students have an opportunity _____

10. The effect of the written and spoken argument _____

11. Physical violence and brutality are replaced _____

12. We will repeat our attempts _____

13. We take this road, _____

B. Answer each question with a complete sentence.

Example: What has one particular characteristic in common?
All roads have one particular characteristic in common.

1. What do the roads have in common? _____

2. What do all people do? _____

3. Which goal became dear to every striving individual? _____

4. What do we believe? _____

5. Into what will the students unite? _____

6. Which great goal will the student Community be bound to? _____

7. What is the student for the world? _____

8. How do the roads to peace become? Why? _____

9. What kind of obstacles fill the road to peace? _____

10. How can the obstacles be cleared? _____

11. What will the student realize? _____

12. On whom rests a great responsibility? _____

13. How will the student be? _____

14. Why do students travel to foreign countries? _____

15. Where do they come to? _____

16. How are the students' reactions? _____

17. What are the students' observations? _____

18. What do the students argue about? _____

19. What has proven successful? _____

20. What do we remember? _____

21. Until when will we repeat our attempts? _____

22. What do we want to practice within the walls of the Universe? _____

IX. Commentary on Model

A. Using the key words and phrases from the MODEL COMPOSITION, write your own composition consisting of three paragraphs on a related topic. Make sure there is an **introductory**, a **main** and a **concluding** paragraph.

roads	people	different
toward a goal	lasting peace	all nations
road to peace	knowledge	ignorance
filled with obstacles	cleared and widened	constantly moving
future of all life	the student	faithful to ideals
strange people	reactions different	travel
common to all mankind	opportunity to discuss	side-by-side
violence and brutality	communication	understanding
bonds of helplessness	University	Universe
state of peace and love		

B. 1. Write about the **lesson** you've learned from the "Dream."

2. Write about the points you agree with.

3. Write about the points you disagree with.

4. Give an appropriate title to your composition.

X. Composition

A. Select one topic below and write a composition consisting of three paragraphs (**introductory**, **main** and **concluding**).

1. An intelligent person is biased.

2. An educated person has no prejudice..

3. People can achieve more through discussion than by fighting.

4. Having fun is more important than working.

5. Working is more important than having fun.

B.   Write a short **composition** (three paragraphs) about the picture below. Remember to include all composition elements.

Chapter Nine

Types of Composition

Words to remember:

Essay writing:

> *analytical*
> *interpretive*
> *knowledge of subject*
> *careful planning*

Correspondence:

> *formal – informal – business –*
> *heading – inside address – salutation –*
> *body – complimentary close – signature*

Term paper:

> *bibliography card – note card –*
> *outline – title page*

I. Model Composition

A. An Essay on Education

1. From the earliest days of our lives, we are involved, one way or another, in some type of education. As small children, we are taught "right" from "wrong" by our parents. The family circle is our first lesson in getting along with others.

2. When we reach school age, our parents enroll us in a public school. This event begins our "formal" education. It is called "formal" because we learn things in school that our parents were unable to teach us. We learn to read, to write and to count. This "formal" education continues throughout our lifetime regardless of the profession or vocation we select for ourselves.

3. Finally, there is a third type of education that everyone undergoes in one's lifetime. This education is based on the experiences of everyday living. Some people regard this type of education as the most significant. One fact remains true: the education of an individual is a never-ending process.

B. Correspondence

1. *Formal*

> John Q. Citizen
> 782 Sandalwood St.
> San Antonio, TX 78226
> September 21, 1974

The President
The White House
Washington, D. C.

Dear Mr. President:

a. The enclosed headline in our local newspaper is the reason for my writing this letter. It is written without the presumption that my advice is being sought but in the firm belief that as a citizen I may be of help in a small way.

b. This letter is written in a sincere effort to lighten the burdens of the awesome task of the office you have assumed: the task of moral reconstruction, reconciliation and a beginning of a meaningful bipartisan dialogue. All this would be greatly served by your selection of a Democrat as your Vice-Presidential choice.

c. Your selection, I feel, would show the nation that a time of unprece-dented cooperation on the political scene has come, nationally as well as internationally. This act will bring us a new era of reason.

d. In the final analysis, the decision is a difficult one to reach. Each man must decide the course of his own destiny. You, Mr. President, decide not only yours but that of our great nation. Congratulations and best wishes.

Yours very truly,

John Q. Citizen

John Q. Citizen

2. *Writing to a Friend*

August 30, 1974

Dear Jim,

a. *The most unusual thing happened this week in San Antonio. The rains came. We've had ten, yes, ten inches of rain in the last thirty-six hours. It certainly brings relief to the parched grass and other greenery. But the consistent rainfall has also created flash floods all over the city. As you know, we have no drainage, and the streets became rivers in no time at all.*

b. *You should have seen the cars floating in four to five feet of water at the intersection of San Pedro and Hildebrand under the railroad bridge! The drivers were rescued in the nick of time, but the cars were a total loss.*

c. *The downpour brought the only excitement to our otherwise easy-going life. We are all well and hope to hear the same from you. Can't wait for your Christmas visit with us. We are counting the days till your arrival. We all miss you.*

d. *Well, there it is. Best of luck to you, and don't forget to write. Keep well and enjoy yourself.*

As always,

Bill

3. *Applying for a Job*

Newspaper Advertisement: Wanted, English Editor, Southern Pub-
                             lishing Co. Indicate experience and salary
                             expected. Vacancy beginning August 15.
                             Write P.O. Box 547, Reston, Virginia
                             22090

                                        Isaac Salinas
                                        P.O. Box 711
                                        Lackland, A. F. Base
                                        San Antonio, TX 78284
                                        June 18, 1974

Southern Publishing Co.
P. O. Box 547
Reston, Virginia 22090

Gentlemen:

a. I saw your advertisement for English Editor in the *Library Journal*
   of June 6, 1974, and I wish to apply for the position. I have now
   completed three years of military duty with the U. S. Air Force, and
   I could start work in the immediate future.

b. During my term of duty with the Armed Forces I worked for the Information and Education Department. My formal training was in
   journalism and English and I have done a lot of work connected with
   news releases and military publications. I am very interested in editorial work and would like to pursue this line of endeavor. If I get
   the job you advertised, I would expect the salary that usually goes
   with the position of English Editor.

c. I am enclosing a personal data sheet with details about my educa-
   tional background and work experience. I will be glad to furnish
   more information upon request, or come for a personal interview. I
   can be reached at the above address, or by phone at area code 512-
   342-8430, any evening after six o'clock. Expecting your kind reply.

                                        Sincerely,

                                        Isaac Salinas

                                        Isaac Salinas

C.   **Mini-Term Paper**

THE CASE OF THE HOT DOG:

A U. S. Favorite

by

Rachel Maya

1. It is a small sausage of finely chopped and seasoned meat, held in a cylindrical covering;[1] most people call this sausage the Hot Dog. Through the years, the Hot Dog has become a favorite with grownups and children of the U. S. of America. Its great popularity is due to the convenience it offers in its preparation.[2] Without much effort this tasty meal can be prepared for large crowds at big sport events or at sidewalk food stands.

2. The tasty sausage was originally called Hot Dog by the U. S. cartoonist Tad Dorgan in 1909.[3] The name was probably an allusion to the popular belief that sausage was made of dog meat. This sausage is served hot in a long, soft roll, with mustard, relish, etc.[4]

---

[1] *The Funk and Wagnalls Encyclopedia* (New York, N.Y. Unicorn Publishers, Inc., 1952), Vol. 29, p. 10797.

[2] Carl Cook, *The World of the Hot Dog* (Chicago, La Cuisine Publishing Co., 1945), p. 45.

[3] *Webster's New World Dictionary* (New York and Cleveland, The World Publishing Co., 1970), p. 679.

[4] *Ibid.*, p. 679.

D.   **Composition by Degrees**

1. a. Copy the title of the essay. ⎯⎯⎯⎯⎯⎯⎯⎯⎯⎯⎯⎯

    b. Copy the sentence that tells what we learn as children. ⎯⎯⎯⎯⎯

    c. Copy the sentence that tells about our first lesson in "getting along."

2. a. Copy the sentence that tells what happens when we reach "school age." ⎯⎯⎯⎯⎯⎯⎯⎯⎯⎯⎯⎯⎯

b. Copy the sentence that tells why school education is called "formal." _____

_____

c. Copy the sentence that tells what we learn in school. _____

_____

3. a. Copy the phrase that tells us what the **third** type of education is.

_____

b. Copy the sentence that tells what we base the third education on.

_____

c. Copy the sentence that tells what some people think about the third type of education. _____

_____

E.   Exercises

1. The following is a mini-essay on a specific topic. Read carefully, then supply a proper title.

TITLE: _____

Mental health is as important to an individual as his physical strength. The secret of life lies in finding a way whereby the mental and physical can live in harmony within one individual. Only then can a person function without much difficulty and cope with daily problems effectively.

It has been said that the power of meditation gives a person the needed energy to become a well-adjusted individual. Therefore, one must devote a part of one's life concerned with the spiritual aspects of being. One must remember that food provides nourishment for a healthy body, but meditation elevates the spirit.

2. The following letters lack the **inside address**, the **forms of address**, and the **complimentary close**. Read the letters carefully then supply proper **inside address**, the **forms of address**, and an appropriate **complimentary close**. In doing so, identify the nature of the letters.

Rebeca Solomon
927 Mt. Kisco
San Antonio, Texas 78213
September 27, 1974

a. _____

_____

_____

———————————————

———————————————

This is written in response to your ad of September 21, 1974, which appeared in our local newspaper concerning an opening for a position of executive secretary.

I have worked in this line of endeavor for over seven years, and I quit my last position only because my family moved to your city. The experiences of the last seven years have been great, and I feel that I want to continue the same line of work.

At your request, references will be forwarded to you. Attached is a personal data sheet for your convenience. Hoping to hear from you soon.

——————————————— ,

Rebeca Solomon

September 10, 1974

b. ———————————————

Though I haven't written for a long time, I've missed you a lot. I keep wondering how you are and how the world is treating you. Things are generally okay here; I only wish my rheumatism would stop annoying me.
    I do hope you can come for the weekend of October 14th. We will be expecting you.

———————————————

———————————————

II. Words in Context

A.   From the list of words and phrases preceding each section fill in each blank space. You may use a selection more than once. Also, you may use more than one word in one blank space.

1. help   enclosed   Dear   advice   letter
   way   belief   citizen   presumption   local
   reason

_____ Mr. President:

The _____headline in our _____ newspaper is the _____for
my writing this _____ . It is written without the _____that my
_____ is being sought but in the firm _____that as a _____I may be
of _____ in a small _____.

2. burdens   sincere   task   lighten
   presently   reconciliation   moral   bipartisan
   choice   selection   greatly

This letter is written in a _____effort to _____ the
_____ of the awesome _____of the office which you have
_____ assumed; the _____of reconstruction, _____ and
a beginning of a meaningful _____dialogue. All this would be _____
served by your _____of a Democrat as your Vice-Presidential _____ .

3. time   show   selection   cooperation
   nationally   act   political   reason
   era

Your _____ , I feel, would _____the nation that a
_____of unprecedented _____ on the_____ scene has come,
_____as well as internationally. This _____ will bring us a
new _____of _____.

4. man   reach   final   great   congratulations
   destiny   decide   course   decision   wishes

In the _____analysis, the _____is a difficult one to
_____ . Each_____ must decide the _____ of his own
_____. You, Mr. President, _____ not only yours but that of
our_____ nation. _____and best _____.

B. Make the necessary change(s) when you substitute the new element into your sentence.

Example: **She writes** a letter to a friend. (They)
        They write a letter to a friend.

1. a. The most unusual **thing** happened this week. (things)

   _____

   b. **It brings** relief to the grass and greenery. (they)

   _____

   c. The **rain has** created flash floods. (rains)

   _____

   d. **The streets** became rivers. (they)

   _____

2. a. The **drivers were** rescued. (driver)

   _____

   b. The **cars were** a total loss. (car)

   _____

3. a. The downpour brought **the only** excitement. (some)

   _____

   b. **I'm** waiting for your Christmas visit. (we're)

   _____

   c. **We're** counting the days. (she's)

   _____

   d. **We all** miss you. (I)

   _____

III. *Structures (Key words [phrases] for composition)*

A. Use the following key words (phrases) to make complete sentences. You may consult the MODEL COMPOSITION.

> Example: earliest days / we / involved
> From the earliest days we are involved.

1. a. saw / advertisement / *Library Journal* _____

   _____

   b. wish / apply / position _____

   c. have / completed / military duty _____

   _____

   d. start / work / immediate future _____

   _____

2. a. during / term of duty / Armed Forces / worked _____

b. training / was / journalism _____

c. have / a lot / work / with news _____

d. am / interested / editorial work _____

e. like / pursue / endeavor _____

f. get / job / advertised _____

g. expect / salary / goes / position _____

3. a. enclosing / personal data / details _____

b. will / furnish / information / request _____

c. come / personal / interview _____

d. be / reached / address _____

e. expecting / reply _____

B.   Supply the missing **preposition** for each blank space. You may consult MODEL COMPOSITION C.

Example: I can be reached ___(at)___ the above address.

1. It is a small sausage _____ finely chopped meat.
2. It is held _____ a cylindrical covering.
3. _____ the years the Hot Dog has become a favorite _____ grownups and children of the U.S. _____ America.
4. It's popularity is due _____ the convenience it offers _____ its preparation.
5. This tasty meal can be prepared _____ large crowds _____ big sports events or _____ sidewalk food stands.
6. The tasty sausage was originally called Hot Dog _____ the U.S.

cartoonist Tad Dorgan _____1909.

7. The name was an allusion_____the popular belief that
sausage was made _____dog meat.

8. This sausage is served hot _____ a long roll.

IV. *Grammar and Syntax [Points of Interest]*

A.   **Essay** writing requires the student to follow three basic steps:

1. decide what type of essay it is to be—**analytical** (determining the nature of an object), or **interpretive** (explaining the nature of an object).

2. have a **detailed knowledge** of the subject.

3. **plan** carefully and write with clarity without repetition and waste.

There is no rule governing the length of an essay. Usually, when there is nothing more to say about the **selected** topic, the essay ends.
Example: (Analytical essay)

On Playing Chess

Chess is played on a checkerboard set. The black corner is to the player's left. The pieces are arranged on the first and second rank facing each opponent. Each piece will face a piece of equal rank across the board. There are two sets of pieces: black and white. Each consists of a King, a Queen, a Bishop, a Rook (or Castle), a Knight and eight Pawns. The white Queen will be on white; black Queen on black. The board is the field of battle in a chess game.

Black

White

[NOTE: Because the King is designated "K" on the board, the Knight goes by the letter "N."]

The King is the most important chess piece. The game ends when the King is captured; this is called "checkmate." Usually, the King is the largest piece on the board.

The Queen is the most powerful chess piece. She is the second largest piece on the board. The Bishop wears a hat and is usually a little smaller than the Queen. The Rook (Castle) resembles a tower. He is usually as tall as the Knight. The Knight resembles the head of a horse. He is important in the game, because he is the only piece that can jump over the other pieces.

Finally, there is the Pawn, the foot soldier. He is the smallest of the chess pieces. However, when the Pawn reaches the opposite side of the board he can become a Queen, a Rook, a Bishop, or a Knight.

Movements of the different pieces vary. The **King** moves one square in any direction.[1] He must not move into a square where he would be in "check" for he might be captured by an enemy piece. When the King is attacked, he must defend himself by moving out of danger ("check"). If the King cannot escape his attacker(s) and he is lost, it is "checkmate," and the game is lost. The **Rook** moves back and forth, left and right, on a straight line. He can go as many squares as he chooses as long as he does not jump other pieces. The **Bishop** moves back and forth on the diagonal line as many squares as he chooses as long as he does not jump other pieces. The Bishop always remains on the field he occupied at the beginning of the game: black or white. The **Queen** can move like the Bishop or the Rook—any place in a straight or diagonal line as long as she does not jump other pieces. The **Knight** moves two squares in one direction and one square at right angles. He can jump over his own or his opponent's men. The **Pawn** moves forward one square at a time except on his first move when he can move two squares forward. The Pawn can capture his opponent diagonally one square to the left or right.

---

[1] Illustrations of the various movements follow the essay.

King Movement

Rook Movement

Bishop Movement

Knight Movement

Queen Movement

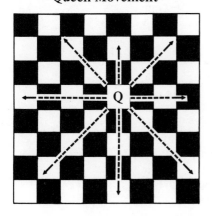

Pawn Movement

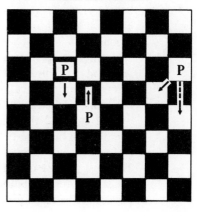

## B.	Correspondence

1. A **formal** letter is usually written to someone not intimately known. It is written for reasons of introducing oneself or one's thoughts regarding a specific question. In writing a formal letter, one should always keep in mind the position of the person to whom the letter is addressed. The letter should be written in a sincere, easy-going and natural manner. The impression the writer will make upon the person to whom the letter is written depends to a great extent upon the appearance, form and tone of the letter.

The following is a sample of a formal (personal) letter:

a. (The **heading** gives the **date** and the full address of the writer.)

John Q. Public, Ph.D.
222 Shadwell Dr.
San Antonio, TX 78228
September 21, 1928

b. The Honorable John Tower
United States Senate
Washington, D. C.

(The **inside address** contains the name and postal address of the person to whom the letter is written.)

c. My dear Senator:

(The **salutation** addresses itself to the person receiving the letter. It sets the tone of the letter.)

d.   It has long been my understanding that all citizens are regarded as equals under the laws of our nation. Recent developments in Washington lead me to believe that my view has been based on a myth or mere speculation.

I am writing to you, as my representative voice in the affairs of our country, to act in rectifying some deficiencies of our judicial system. All citizens are counting on the honesty and sincerity of some public figures. The trust we have placed in your hands is a responsibility, not a privilege to be taken for granted.

(The **body** of the letter tells in simple, short sentences the thoughts the writer wishes to make known to the person for whom the letter is intended.)

e. Yours very truly,

  John Q. Public

(The **complimentary close** should be appropriate to the person(s) addressed.)

f. John Q. Public, Ph.D.

(The written **signature** is placed between the complimentary close and the writer's **typed** name.)

2. An **informal** letter is usually written to someone intimately known. It tells about people and events with which the writer and the person to whom the letter is addressed are familiar. One writes an informal letter when one feels the need to **converse** with another person. The letter, therefore, is more like a conversation than a formality; it is **sincere, original** and **easy-going**. It is usually written in **longhand**. The example is a letter inviting a friend to visit and attend a concert.

San Antonio, September 21, 1974

My dear Rosi,

Though I wrote you last night, there was one item I forgot to mention; this Friday night there is a guest concert of the Boston Pops at the City Auditorium. I bought two reserved seat tickets a month ago, so this is to invite you to come and spend the entire weekend with us. You've always wanted to hear this famous orchestra, and now you'll have the opportunity to do so.

After a week long fight with the flu, I'm finally getting better. Hopefully, by the time you get here I'll be well. Please call to let me know if you decide not to come. If I don't hear from you before Friday, I'll assume that you'll be here for the concert. See you soon.

Love,

Bill

REPLY:

Houston, September 23, 1974

Dear Bill,

I was sorry to hear about your illness, but happy to learn that you are almost well. Of course, I'll be delighted to visit with you for the weekend. I'm looking forward to the concert. It's a real treat! Just what I've always dreamed about. See you Friday. Thanks.

Love,

Rosi

3. A **business** letter that is written with clarity tells in a **direct** manner what it is that the writer wants. The writing must also be **polite** and **natural** because it will tell the person(s) who will receive it much about the writer's character and personality.

Example:

April 15, 1974   **(date)**

William W. Flower   (The **heading** gives first the **date**
P. O. Box 1145   then the full address of the
Stamford, Conn. 06904   writer.)

Director of Sales   (The **inside address** gives the title
Meridian Publishers   and the full address of the
P. O. Box 1495   person to whom the letter is
San Antonio, Texas 78284   written.)

Dear Sir: **(Salutation)**

It has been one year and several   (The **body** of the letter tells
months since the publication of   clearly, in ordinary English, the
my book *Technical Swahili* and   writer's reason of forwarding the
there has been no quarterly sales   letter.)
report sent to me.

This letter is written to inquire
about the total number of sold
copies thus far. You will find
the clause covering this require-
ment on page three of our Publication Agreement.

Hoping to hear from you soon.

Sincerely yours,   (The **complimentary close** must
                  be appropriate to the person re-

William W. Flower	ceiving the letter.)
William W. Flower	(The **signature** is written in hand above the **typed** signature.)

C. Term (Research) Paper

A **term (research) paper** is simply a composition assignment. The term paper is usually longer than any other written assignment. The student selects the **main idea** for the paper, but the paper itself is based on what others have said about the subject. Therefore, a term paper requires **research.**

1. *Bibliography Card*—Research is carried out because facts are needed for the term paper. Each source of information must be recorded on a separate **bibliography card**. The collected bibliography cards will later serve as **footnotes** and bibliography. There are many types of bibliography cards. Here are examples of two such cards:

a. A book by **one author**:

Author	Mostar, Gerhart Herrmann
Title	*A Critical Profile*
Essential Data (give page unless the entire book was read)	The Hague, Mouton, n.v. Publishers, 1968

b. A book with **no author's name** given:

Title	*Webster's New World Dictionary*
Essential Data	New York and Cleveland, The World Publishing Company, 1970, p. 121

For more information about arranging footnotes and bibliographies the teacher will inform the students which **style manual** the students will use.

2. *Note Card*—It is important to take good **notes** when additional sources are found and consulted. The notes should be written clearly on cards similar to those for bibliography. The note is a **summary** of the source material, or a direct quote, which will be included directly in the paper.

The following is a sample note card:

Heading

Source

Notes and page reference in
left margin

> *The Lively Art, Payne*
> *200 "A note may be a summary*
> *in your own words of an au-*
> *thor's meaning or it may be*
> *a quotation taken directly*
> *from his work. If it is a quo-*
> *tation, it must be **exactly** as*
> *it appears in print and must*
> *be enclosed in quotation*
> *marks."*

The following is a **bibliography card** for the preceding **note card**.

Author

Title

Essential Data

> Payne, Lucile Vaughan
>
> *The Lively Art of Writing*
>
> Chicago, Follet Educational Cor-
> poration, 1965, p. 14.

After all notes are taken the student is ready to write the paper. Certain
steps should be followed in writing the term paper.

a. Arrange **note cards** according to subject. Cards with information
about the same subject must be together.

b. Prepare an **outline** following the **note card** arrangement.

c. Write the **first draft** of the paper.

d. **Reread** and **revise** the composition carefully.

D.   The **title page** presents a short, general statement containing information
about the paper. The following is a sample TITLE PAGE:

THE VARIOUS WAYS OF

PREPARING SALADS

by

Katinka Mostar

Chemistry 406, Hour 5

May 3, 1974

E.   Exercises

1. Following are samples of **bibliography cards**. Examine them carefully and identify the missing item(s).

   a. A book by one author:

   > Croft, Kenneth (Editor)
   >
   > *Readings on English as a*
   > *Second Language.*
   >
   >   Winthrop Publisher, Inc.

   b. A book with no author's name given:

   > *The Columbia Viking Desk Encyclopedia*
   >
   > New York, Viking Press

2. Arrange the "steps" for term paper writing in their proper order.

    a. Write the first draft of the paper.   _____

    b. Arrange note cards according to subject.   _____

    c. Reread and revise the composition.   _____

    d. Prepare an outline.   _____

V. *Idea Recognition*

Copy from MODEL COMPOSITION (I.A.) the sentences expressing:

A. when our involvement in education begins . . .

_____

B. what we are taught as small children . . .

_____

C. what our first lesson in getting along with others is . . .

_____

D. what our parents do when we reach school age . . .

_____

E. what the enrollment in school begins . . .

_____

F. when education is called "formal" . . .

_____

G. how long "formal" education continues . . .

_____

H. what the third type of education is . . .

_____

I. what we base this education on . . .

_____

J. how some people regard this education . . .

_____

K. what fact remains true . . .

_____

VI. *Vocabulary Enrichment*

A. **Paraphrasing**

The following are **paraphrases** (rephrasing expressions or words without changing their meaning) of expressions or words found in the narrative. Write the expressions found in the MODEL COMPOSITION (B.1.) which correspond the paraphrases below.

> Example: our local newspaper
> **a newspaper published locally**

1. that's why I'm writing _____

_____

2. I don't suppose you want my advice _____

_____

3. I strongly believe I can help _____

_____

4. I sincerely want to help _____

_____

5. the job of moral change _____

_____

6. of making up _____

_____

7. beginning a two-party conversation _____

_____

8. it would help to get a Democrat Vice-President _____

_____

9. a cooperation as it never before existed _____

_____

10. not only at home, but also abroad _____

_____

11. after all, it's tough to make up your mind _____

_____

12. everyone has to decide what he wants to do _____

_____

B.   Lexical Units

Select the word (phrase) from the following list that best completes each of the sentences below. You may use a selection more than once.

> Example: From the earliest days of our lives **we are learning** right from wrong. We are **involved** in **some type of education**.

| "formal" | teach | get along |
| process | experience | each day |

1. The **family circle** is our **first lesson**. We learn to _____with others.

2. When we reach school age, we **attend public school**. This event begins our _____ education.

3. We **learn many things** in school. Our parents were unable to _____ us those things.

4. The "formal" education **continues throughout** our lifetime. Education is a never ending _____ .

5. What we **learn** in **life** is important too. We call this _____ .

6. **Experience** is a significant **part** of education. We add to this type of education _____   _____ .

C.   Related Words

Use related words to rewrite the following sentences without changing their meanings. Change the underlined word. Make further changes if necessary.

Example: involved (v.)   involvement (n.)
We are **involved** in education.
Education **is an involvement.**

health (n.)	mental (adj.)	physical (adj.)
healthy (adj.)	mentally (adv.)	physically (adv.)
meditation (n.)	to adjust (v.)	to elevate (v.)
to meditate (v.)	adjusted (adj.)	elevating (adj.)
effective (adj.)		
effectively (adv.)		

1. It is important for an individual to be mentally **healthy**. _____
_____

2. A person must find a way to harmonize **mentally** and **physically**. _____
_____

3. One must find an **effective** way to function and cope with daily problems. _____
_____

4. When we **meditate**, we get the needed energy. _____
_____

5. He is a well-**adjusted** individual. _____

_____

6. Meditation is **elevating** to the spirit. _____

_____

VII. Steps in Writing

A. Add new words and revise the sentence to suit the changes indicated in parentheses.

> Example: Food provides nourishment for **the body**. (us)
> Food provides nourishment for **us**.

1. **This is written** in response to your ad. (I am writing)

_____

2. The ad appeared **in our newspaper**. (there)

_____

3. **I have** worked as a secretary for seven years. (she)

_____

4. **I quit my** last position because I was ill. (he)

_____

5. **My family** moved to your city. (we)

_____

6. **I feel** that **I want** to continue. (she)

_____

7. At **your** request, **references** will be forwarded. (his, they)

_____

8. Attached **is a** personal data **sheet** for you. (are)

_____

B. Opposites

Use the opposites to rewrite the following sentences. Make the necessary changes to suit the new sentences. You may use a word more than once.

> Example: least—most
> The King is the **least** important chess piece.
> The King is the **most** important chess piece.

| largest | smaller | most | capture(d) |

always	important	smallest	tall
opponent	lost	beginning	different

1. The game ends when the King is **liberated**. _____

   _____

2. Usually, the King is the **smallest** piece on the board. _____

   _____

3. The Queen is the **least** powerful chess piece. _____

   _____

4. She is the second **smallest** piece on the board. _____

   _____

5. The Bishop is usually a little **larger** than the Queen. _____

   _____

6. The Rook is usually as **short** as the Knight. _____

   _____

7. The Knight is **unimportant** in the game. _____

   _____

8. The Pawn is the **largest** of the pieces. _____

   _____

9. Movements of the **same** pieces vary. _____

   _____

10. When the King cannot escape, the game is **won**. _____

    _____

11. The Bishop **never** remains on the field he occupied in the **end** of the game. _____

    _____

12. The Pawn can **liberate** his opponent diagonally. _____

    _____

13. The Pawn can capture his **friend**. _____

    _____

VIII.   *Comprehension*

A.   Complete the sentence and add as many related sentences as you can find in the MODEL COMPOSITION (I.A.).

   Example: The King is the most important **chess piece**.

The game ends when the King is captured; this is called "checkmate."

1. From the earliest days _____

_____

_____

2. As small children, _____

_____

_____

3. When we reach school age, _____

_____

_____

4. It is called "formal" because _____

_____

_____

5. This "formal" education continues _____

_____

_____

6. Finally, there is a third type _____

_____

_____

7. Some people regard this type _____

_____

_____

8. One fact remains true: _____

_____

_____

B.   Reply with complete sentences. MODEL COMPOSITION (B.2.).

Example: What happened in San Antonio?
The most unusual thing happened.

1. What came to San Antonio? _____

_____

2. How many inches of rain were there? _____

_____

3. For how many hours did the rain fall? _____

_____

4. What does the rain bring? _____

5. What did the rainfall create? ⸻

6. Why did the streets become rivers? ⸻

7. Where were the cars floating? ⸻

8. Why did the cars float? ⸻

9. What was situated above the flooded streets? ⸻

10. How were the drivers rescued? ⸻

11. What happened to the cars? ⸻

12. What did the downpour bring? ⸻

13. How is life in San Antonio? ⸻

14. How is the writer of the letter? ⸻

15. What does the writer wait for? ⸻

16. What is the writer counting? ⸻

17. What does the writer wish for Jim? ⸻

IX. *Commentary on Model*

A. Using the key words and phrases from the MODEL COMPOSITION (E.1.), write a short composition on a related topic. Be sure to supply three bibliography cards containing sentences used in your composition. Give your composition an appropriate title.

mental health	secret of life
physical strength	live in harmony
function without much difficulty	cope with problems
power of meditation	gives needed energy
well-adjusted	be concerned with the spiritual
nourishment of body	elevate the spirit
individual	person

B. 1. Write about the **lesson** you've learned from MODEL COMPOSITION 1.A.

2. Write about the points you agree with.

3. Write about the points you disagree with.

4. Give an appropriate title to your composition.

X. *Composition*

A. 1. Prepare five **bibliography cards** of books you select.

2. Prepare five **note cards** from the above books.

B. Select one topic below and write a short (100 words) paper about it. Remember to include **bibliography** cards, **note** cards, and an **outline**.

1. jazz music

2. skyscrapers

3. cowboys

4. silent movies

5. "the most typical thing I know about my country"

6. American music

7. American architecture

C. Rewrite the letter in E.2.b. in the **we** person. Make all appropriate changes.

D.   Describe the activities of the individuals in the picture below.

Chapter Ten

Style, Form and Structure

Words to remember:

Style: Formal–Informal

Simplicity – Sincerity – Directness

Form

Poetry   *Prose*

Letters   *Dialogue*

Shape

Triangle   *Square*

Circle   *Pentagon*

odd shapes

Structure

simple sentence – compound sentence
beginning – middle – end
introduction – body – conclusion

I. Model Composition

A.   Style is What You Make of It

1. Everyone has heard of "Ernest, the show off." From his flashy Cadillac convertible down to the polished tips of his expensive shoes, Ernest pretended to know how to live and spend his money. This was his style. His friends said that Ernest invented the expression "life style" so that others would imitate him. But that was only hearsay.

2. The truth was, no one really wanted to imitate Ernest. The language he used was like his flashy personality. He used cheap, vulgar words, even when he attempted to describe simple events. He was unable to think simply and directly. He lacked orderliness and sincerity.

3. Ernest did not realize that all his flashiness and money spending were fruitless habits. He tried in vain to impress those who would stay and listen to him till early morning hours. Ernest began to suspect that his "friends" stayed with him only to amuse themselves. The more aware Ernest became that his suspicions were true, the less capable he was of controlling his habits. Soon, because of the excessive spending, Ernest became a poor man.

4. It was only then that Ernest recognized the foolish ways of his past. He began reading with a passion. His job allowed him to spend his afternoons in the public library, where he became a familiar figure to all who worked there. His desire for knowledge was endless, as though he wished to make up for all the years of intellectual inactivity.

5. The change Ernest underwent was obvious. He dressed modestly and learned to be orderly and sincere. The economy car he drove was sufficient means of transportation. He became thrifty and less generous in spending his money foolishly. Ernest had fewer friends now, but those he had did not secretly amuse themselves at his expense. As his values changed, so did his style.

B.   Composition by Degrees

1. a. Copy the phrase that tells about Ernest's character. _____

   _____

   b. Copy the sentence that tells what Ernest pretended to know. _____

   _____

   c. Copy the phrase Ernest "invented."_____

   _____

2. a. Copy the sentence that tells how Ernest talked. _____

   _____

   b. Copy the sentence that tells what Ernest lacked. _____

   _____

3. a. Copy the sentence that tells about Ernest's habits. _____
_____

   b. Copy the sentence that tells what Ernest tried in vain._____
_____

   c. Copy the sentence that tells why Ernest's friends stayed with him. ____
_____

   d. Copy the sentence that tells why Ernest was "less capable of controlling his habits." _____
_____

   e. Copy the sentence that tells why Ernest became poor. _____
_____

4. a. Copy the sentence that tells what Ernest recognized. _____
_____

   b. Copy the sentence that tells where Ernest spent his afternoons. _____
_____

   c. Copy the sentence that tells to whom Ernest became a "familiar figure."
_____

   d. Copy the phrase that tells about Ernest's "desire for knowledge." ____
_____

5. a. Copy the sentence that tells how Ernest dressed. _____
_____

   b. Copy the phrase that tells what type of car Ernest drove. _____
_____

   c. Copy the phrase that tells what the car was for Ernest. _____
_____

   d. Copy the phrases that tell how Ernest became in spending. _____
_____

   e. Copy the sentence that tells how his friends were. _____
_____

II. Words in Context

A.   From the list of words preceding each section fill in each blank space. You
may use a selection more than once. Also, you may use more than one word in
one blank space.

1. expensive	polished	pretended	heard
style	said	others	imitate
flashy	hearsay	spend	invented

Everyone has _____ of "Ernest, the show off." From his _____
Cadillac convertible, on down to the_____tips of his _____ shoes, Ernest
_____ to know how to live and _____ his money. This was his
_____. His friends _____ that Ernest _____ the expression "life style"
so that _____ would _____ him. But this was only_____ .

	2. wanted	cheap	language	truth
	flashy	simple	attempted	unable
	orderliness	directly	sincerity	

The _____ was, no one really_____ to imitate Ernest. The _____
he used was like his _____ personality. He used _____ , vulgar words, even
when he _____ to describe_____ events. He was _____ to think simply and
_____ . He lacked _____and _____ .

	3. aware	suspect	realize	flashiness
	suspicions	amuse	morning	fruitless
	excessive	poor	controlling	less
	impress	listen		

Ernest did not _____that all his _____ and money spending were
_____ habits. He tried in vain to _____those who would stay and
_____ to him till early_____hours. Ernest began to _____that
his "friends" stayed with him only to_____themselves. The more
_____Ernest became that his _____ were true, the_____ capable he was of
_____his habits. Soon, because of his_____ spending, Ernest became
a _____man.

	4. ways	public	reading	recognized
	desire	familiar	allowed	passion
	endless	make up	intellectual	

It was only then Ernest _____ the foolish _____of his past. He began
_____with a_____. His job_____him to spend his afternoons in the_____
library, where he became a _____ figure to all who worked there. His
_____ for knowledge was_____, as though he wished to _____ _____
for all the years of_____inactivity.

	5. modestly	drove	orderly	change	generous
	means	thrifty	sincere	underwent	foolishly
	style	secretly	expense	friends	values

The _____which Ernest _____was obvious. He dressed _____and
learned to be _____ and _____ . The economy car he_____was a

sufficient _____ of transportation. He became _____ and less _____
in spending his money _____. Ernest had fewer _____ now, but those he
had did not _____ amuse themselves at his _____. As his _____ changed,
so did his _____ .

B. Make the necessary change(s) when you substitute the new element into
your sentence.

> Example: Style is what **you** make of it. (they)
> Style is what **they** make of it.

1. a. **Everyone has** heard of "Ernest the show off." (They)
   _____

   b. **Ernest** pretended to know how to live. (she)
   _____

   c. This was **his** style. (our)
   _____

2. a. No one really wanted to imitate **Ernest**. (me)
   _____

   b. The language **he** used was flashy. (I)
   _____

   c. **He was** unable to think simply and directly. (we)
   _____

3. a. **His** flashiness and spending were fruitless habits. (their)
   _____

   b. **He** tried to impress **his** friends. (I)
   _____

   c. **He** was unable to control **his** habits. (she)
   _____

   d. Soon, **Ernest** became a poor **man**. (she)
   _____

4. a. **Ernest** recognized the foolish ways of **his** past. (we)
   _____

   b. **His** job allowed **him** to read many books. (my)
   _____

   c. **His** desire for knowledge was endless. (her)
   _____

   d. **He** wished to make up for all the years of intellectual inactivity. (I)
   _____

III.   *Structures (Key words [phrases] for composition)*

A.   Use the following key words (phrases) to make complete sentences. You may consult the MODEL COMPOSITION.

      Example: style / what / make / it
              Style is what you make of it.

1. a. everyone / heard / Ernest _____

   b. flashy convertible / expensive shoes / Ernest / pretended his / style

   c. friends / said / Ernest / invented / "life style" _____

   d. this / was / hearsay _____

2. a. no one / wanted / imitate _____

   b. Ernest / language / used / flashy _____

   c. he / used / vulgar / attempted / simple events _____

   d. he / unable / think / simply / directly _____

   e. he / lacked / orderliness / sincerity _____

3. a. Ernest / realize / flashiness / fruitless habits _____

   b. he / tried / in vain / impress _____

   c. friends / stayed / amuse / themselves _____

   d. he / unable / controlling / habits _____

   e. Ernest / became / poor _____

4. a. only / then / Ernest / recognized / foolish ways _____

b. began / reading / passion _____

_____

c. job / allowed / spend / afternoons / library _____

_____

d. became / familiar figure / to all / worked _____

_____

e. desire / knowledge / endless _____

_____

f. wished / make up / the years / inactivity _____

_____

5. a. change / Ernest / underwent / obvious _____

_____

b. dressed / modestly / learned / be / orderly _____

_____

c. economy / car / drove / means / transportation ____

_____

d. became / thrifty / less generous _____

_____

e. Ernest / fewer / friends _____

_____

f. values / changed / did / style _____

_____

B. Supply the missing **preposition** for each blank space. You may consult the MODEL COMPOSITION.

Example: Style is what you make ___(of)___ it.

1. Everyone has heard _____ "Ernest, the show off."
2. _____ his flashy Cadillac convertible, on down _____ the polished tips _____ his expensive shoes, Ernest pretended to know how to live.
3. He tried to impress those who would listen _____ him.
4. His friends stayed _____ him to amuse themselves.
5. Soon, _____ the excessive spending, Ernest became a poor man.
6. He recognized the foolish ways _____ his past.
7. He began reading _____ a passion.

8. He spent his afternoons _____ the Public Library.

9. Ernest became a familiar figure _____ all.

10. His desire _____ knowledge was endless.

11. He wished to make up _____ all the years of intellectual inactivity.

12. The car was a means _____ transportation.

13. He was less generous _____ spending.

14. They did not amuse themselves _____ his expense.

IV. Grammar and Syntax [Points of Interest]

A. Style

This book has guided the student through the initial steps of learning how to write. **Style, form** and **structure** are considered the finer points of writing.

Language changes from day to day. Words assume new meaning under different circumstances. Two commonly known levels of usage are Standard English (formal and informal) and sub-standard English (slang). Standard English is the kind of language spoken and written by most educated people in English-speaking countries. Sub-standard English is the language spoken in less educated social circles. Therefore, before experimenting with words and their varied usage, the student should try to follow the basic principles of Standard English.

Style varies from writer to writer, from one period to another, and from one subject matter to another. It is generally agreed that the most effective style of writing is demonstrated with **simplicity, sincerity** and **directness.** The simpler and more direct the writing, the easier it is for the reader to follow and understand it. Effective writing does not rely on tricks or adornments. It should be thrifty. The following thought expresses what is meant by "thrifty" writing:

WORDS

If I could express a thought in one word,
I would refuse to use more . .
Were I able to cut down a tree at one stroke,
I would strike but once . .
but
When running the risk of being misunderstood,
or leaving things unaccomplished,
I would spare neither words nor deeds . . .

From the style of the following excerpts, the reader should be able to identify their source:

1. And Pharoah said unto Joseph: "See, I have set thee over all the land of Egypt." And Pharoah took off his signet ring from his hand, and put it upon Joseph's hand, and arrayed him in vestures of fine linen, and put a gold chain about his neck. And he made him to ride in the second chariot which he had; and they cried before him: "Abrech"; and he set him over all the land of Egypt. And Pharoah said unto Joseph: "I am Pharaoh, and without thee shall no man lift up his hand or his foot in all the land of Egypt."

GENESIS, 41:44

2. THE FOX AND THE LION

One day a fox who had never seen a lion was walking in the woods. Suddenly the king of beasts stood in the path before him, and the fox almost died of fright. He ran away and hid himself in his den. The next time he came upon the lion he merely paused to allow the majestic beast to pass by. The third time they met, the fox boldly approached the lion and passed the time of day with him and asked after his family's health.

APPLICATION: FAMILIARITY BREEDS CONTEMPT.

Aesop's Fables

3. When in the course of human events, it becomes necessary for one people to dissolve the political bonds which have connected them with another, and to assume among the powers of the earth, the separate and equal station to which the Laws of Nature and of Nature's God entitle them, a decent respect to the opinions of mankind requires that they should declare the causes which impel them to the separation.
---------We hold these truths to be self-evident, that all men are created equal, that they are endowed by their Creator with certain unalienable Rights, that among these are Life, Liberty and the pursuit of Happiness.----------

In Congress, July 4, 1776
The Unanimous Declaration of the
Thirteen United States of America

B. Form and Structure

Form and **structure** are related; they are blood cousins. Furthermore, they cannot be separated from **style**, directly or indirectly. After deciding on a topic, the writer must make up his mind about the **form** of his writing. Is it going to be a **poem**? Is it better to express the thoughts and ideas in **prose** (narrative) form? Some writers have selected to write entire novels in the form of an **exchange** of **letters** between the characters. Others prefer the form of **dialogue**. There are many forms of writing. The most popular form is **prose** because it seems the easiest way to express thoughts clearly.

No matter what the form of a composition may be, to be complete it will have a **beginning** (introduction), a **middle** (body) and an **end** (conclusion); this is called the **structure** of writing. How **long** or how **short** a sentence is may also be regarded as the structure of writing. Simple, declarative sentences will be easier to understand, or to write, than the more complicated sentences.

Form is to writing what **shape** is to **space**. We have familiar shapes:

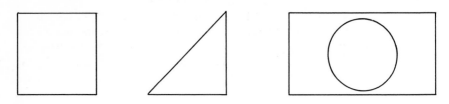

and we have some unfamiliar shapes:

Whenever the form of writing becomes unfamiliar, it is more difficult to understand than the more popular way of expressing the **same** thought.

Examples:

(Poetry)

A GEM
A gem loses its value in its abundance,
so does a word when misused --

demand and value are conversely consistent,
they both decrease when abused . . .

(Prose)   *A GEM*
When there are too many gems, they are worthless,
because the more we have of something, the less
we appreciate it. The same rule applies to words:
they are worthless when they are misused.

The following are two ways of expressing the **same** thought; the first is in the form of poetry, the second as a composite of shapes and words.

1.   *LIVE FOR DEATH . . .*

smoke . . . smoke . . . smoke . . .
fog . . . fog . . . fog . . .
smog . . . smog . . . smog . . .
pollution . . .
*   suffocation . . .*
slow death . . .

danger is the staff
of life for
the new generation . . .

desperately seeking
nirvana, the magic wand
called weed . . . acid . . . LSD . . .

forgetting . . .

pollution . . . suffocation . . .
a gradual, but certain
escape in death . . .

2.   *LIVE FOR DEATH*

C. Exercises

1. Following are short excerpts composed in different **styles** of writing. Indicate which of the passages is written in **formal** and which in **informal** English.

    a. Several nights ago, we went out to hear a musical performance. I was ill at ease and could not quite adjust to the situation. I did get to enjoy the evening eventually because the musicians were delightful. _____

    b. A couple of nights past, we got to go to a musical show. I didn't feel good. It was like I didn't fit into it. But finally I did have a good time because the music was great. _____

    c. Mary sat near the window contemplating the landscape. The sun was setting on the horizon, there was generally no noise coming from the outdoors, and the children were in bed for the night. Although she had never been to Europe, Mary would have liked to visit with her relatives there. They had not seen each other for over two years. However, with all the household duties and financial obligations, the outlook for an extensive vacation in the near future seemed very unlikely. She sighed heavily. _____

    d. Mary was sitting near the window thinking about the outdoors. It was sundown. It was quiet out there. The children were already bedded down for the night. Though she'd never been to Europe, she'd like to pay a visit to her relatives there. But she had too many things to do at home. With all her obligations, she couldn't see making plans for a long vacation. There'd be no chance for that soon. She felt sorry for herself. _____

2. Following are examples of several **forms** of writing. Indicate the **form** of writing for each of the examples. Rewrite examples a, b, c and d in **narrative** form.

    a.   SENSATIONS
          To experience sensations and feel
          emotions of the **other** sex
          is like trying to sense the desperation
          of a sparkling snowflake as it
          melts upon a warm surface . . .

b.   THE RING
women are the diamonds, men
the platinum which lends them support—
united they ornament one another,
apart, their purpose seems vague .. rather . . .

c.   THE LIE
the truth spoken meekly
is less convincing than
a brightly colored lie
shouted from the rooftops . . .

d.   VIRTUE
man's virtue lies not in his
recognition of the false
but in the service of the true . . .

e.   HALFWAY MARK
enough enthusiasm in
any endeavor is a halfway
mark to achievement . . .

f.   A FRAGMENT
The girl fought quietly but desperately against his searching, strong
fingers. Forster held her tightly with one arm around her slim waist.
With the other, he bent her over backward till she was prostrate on
top of the crate. The crate squeaked treacherously under the weight,
and Bronia continued in her attempt to escape from under Forster's
massive frame. Within the next few moments, in the quivering light
of the furnace we observed the most mystifying proceedings.[1]

g.

"Roman, Menasha was right," I whispered, "we build and they
destroy. Now we destroy as well. We *are* like them!"

"Don't be a fool. We fight the best way we know how," Roman
replied.

"It's not that simple," I insisted. "Seems like everything is crazy
and we are at the center of it!"

"Yes, so?" My brother cut off the discussion.

---

[1]Samelson, William. *All Lie in Wait*. Englewood Cliffs, N.J., Prentice-Hall, Inc.,
1969, p. 87.

"Good-bye, Tuviah!"
"Take care, Pinhas!"[2]

V. *Idea Recognition*

Copy from the MODEL COMPOSITION the sentences expressing:

A. who has heard of Ernest . . .

B. what kind of a car Ernest drove . . .

C. what kind of shoes Ernest wore . . .

D. what Ernest pretended to know . . .

E. which expression Ernest was supposed to have invented . . .

F. why others would imitate Ernest . . .

G. what kind of language Ernest used . . .

H. how Ernest's personality was . . .

I. what Ernest's personality was compared to . . .

J. why Ernest was unable to think simply and directly . . .

K. what Ernest did not realize . . .

L. whom Ernest tried to impress . . .

M. why his friends stayed with Ernest . . .

N. when Ernest became less capable of controlling his habits . . .

O. why Ernest became a poor man . . .

---

[2]*Ibid.*, p. 211.

P.   when Ernest recognized the foolish ways of his past . . .

_____

Q.   what his job allowed him to do . . .

_____

R.   to whom Ernest became a familiar figure . . .

_____

S.   how his desire for knowledge was . . .

_____

T.   why his desire for knowledge was so great . . .

_____

U.   what was obvious . . .

_____

V.   how Ernest dressed . . .

_____

W.   what Ernest drove . . .

_____

X.   how Ernest became . . .

_____

Y.   how his friends were . . .

_____

VI.   Vocabulary Enrichment

A.   Paraphrasing

The following are **paraphrases** (rephrasing expressions or words without changing their meanings) of expressions or words found in the narrative. Write expressions found in the MODEL COMPOSITION which correspond to the paraphrases below.

Example: a way of life — **style**

1. a boastful person _____

_____

2. a very fancy car _____

_____

3. he made believe _____

_____

4. others would do the same _____

5. not really the truth _____

6. he tried to talk about things _____

7. only to make fun _____

8. to do what he wished _____

9. he spent more than he had _____

10. everybody knew him _____

11. he wanted to learn _____

12. for lack of learning _____

13. the car took him places _____

14. he saved money _____

15. not as many friends _____

B.　Lexical Units

Select the word (phrase) from the following list that best completes each of the sentences below. You may use a selection more than once.

Example: Ernest drove a **flashy** car. He was a **show off**.

imitate	cheap	style	vulgar
orderliness	controlling	excessive	amused
reading	sufficient	familiar	hearsay
impress			

1. Ernest **pretended to know how to live**. That was his _____

2. They **said** that he invented the expression "life style." But that was

only _____ .

3. He wanted people to do the **same** as he did. But no one really wanted to _____ his style.

4. The language he used was like his **flashy personality**. The words were _____ and _____ .

5. He was unable to **think simply**. He lacked _____ .

6. He **spent** a lot of money. Ernest tried to _____ his friends.

7. His friends **listened** and **laughed**. They _____ themselves.

8. The more **aware** he became of his friends' behavior, the less capable he was of _____ his habits.

9. Ernest became a **poor** man. This happened because of _____ spending.

10. Ernest had a **desire** to **learn**. He began _____ with a passion.

11. He **spent** many **hours in the library**. Ernest became a _____ figure to those who worked there.

12. He bought a **small** car. It was _____ means of transportation.

C. Related Words

Use related words to rewrite the following sentences without changing their meaning. Change the underlined word(s). Make further changes if necessary.

Example: to make (v.)   making (n.)
Style is what you **make** of it.
Style is of your own **making**.

to invent (v.) invention (n.)	to imitate (v.) imitation (n.)	to use (v.) use (n.)
to attempt (v.) attempt (n.)	orderliness (n.) orderly (adj.)	sincerity (n.) sincere (adj.)
to amuse (v.) amusing (adj.)	to desire (v.) desire (n.)	to spend (v.) spending (n.)
to suspect (v.) suspicion (n.) suspicious (adj.)	excessively (adv.) excessive (adj.)	

1. Ernest's style was his own **invention**. _____
_____

2. No one wanted to become an **imitation** of Ernest. _____

3. Ernest made **use** of vulgar language. _____

4. He made an **attempt** to think simply. _____

5. He wasn't **orderly** and **sincere.** _____

6. Ernest's ways were flashy and he was **amusing** to friends. _____

7. Ernest **suspected** all his friends. _____

8. He became poor because he would **spend excessively.** _____

9. Ernest **desired** knowledge. _____

VII. *Steps in Writing*

A. Add new words and revise the sentence to suit the changes indicated in parentheses.

> Example: Style is what **you** make of it. (we)
> Style is what **we** make of it.

1. **His** flashy Cadillac was expensive. (my)
_____

2. **Ernest** knew how to spend money. (we)
_____

3. This **was his** style. (has been, my)
_____

4. **His** friends said that **he** invented the expression. (my, I)
_____

5. **He** had a **flashy** personality. (she, good)
_____

6. **He** used **cheap, vulgar** words. (they, nice, exceptional)
_____

7. **He lacked** orderliness and sincerity. (she, enjoyed)
_____

8. **They** listened to **him** till early morning. (we, them)

_____

9. **His friends** amused **themselves**. (we, ourselves)

_____

10. **He** became a poor **man**. (she, woman)

_____

11. **He** began reading many **books**. (I, stories)

_____

12. **He** spent **his** afternoons in the library. (she, her)

_____

13. **His** desire for knowledge was endless. (my)

_____

14. **Ernest** had fewer friends now. (Jane)

_____

15. As **his** values changed, so did **his** style. (my)

_____

B.   Opposites

Use the opposites to rewrite the following sentences. Make the necessary changes to suit the new sentences. You may use a word more than once.

> Example: flashy — modest
> He drove a **modest** car.
> He drove a **flashy** car.

vulgar	dull	spend(ing)	cheap	no one
less	early	lacked	simply	fruitless
poor	fewer	great	foolish(ly)	a lie
capable	sufficient			

1. **Everyone** has heard of Ernest. _____

_____

2. He wore **polished, expensive** shoes. _____

_____

3. Ernest pretended to know how to **save** his money. _____

_____

4. This was **truth**. _____

_____

5. He used **expensive, refined** words. _____

6. He was unable to think **in a complicated way.** _____

7. He **possessed** orderliness and sincerity. _____

8. His flashiness and spending were **fruitful** habits. _____

9. They stayed with him till **late** morning hours. _____

10. He was **incapable** of controlling his habits. _____

11. Soon, he became a **rich** man. _____

12. He recognized his **wise** ways. _____

13. His desire for knowledge was **small.** _____

14. The economy car he drove was **insufficient** means of transportation.

15. He was **more** generous in saving. _____

16. He spent his money **wisely.** _____

17. Ernest had **more** friends now. _____

VIII. *Comprehension*

A. Complete the sentences and add as many related sentences as you can find in the MODEL COMPOSITION.

> Example: From his flashy Cadillac convertible, **down to the polished tips of his expensive shoes, Ernest pretended to know how to live and spend his money.**

1. His friends said that Ernest invented the expression "life style." _____

2. The truth was, —————————————————————

———————————————————————————————

———————————————————————————————

3. He was unable to think ———————————————————

———————————————————————————————

———————————————————————————————

4. Ernest did not realize ————————————————————

———————————————————————————————

———————————————————————————————

5. He tried in vain to impress ———————————————————

———————————————————————————————

———————————————————————————————

6. Ernest began to suspect ————————————————————

———————————————————————————————

———————————————————————————————

7. Soon, because of the excessive spending, ——————————

———————————————————————————————

———————————————————————————————

8. It was only then ——————————————————————

———————————————————————————————

———————————————————————————————

9. His job allowed him ————————————————————

———————————————————————————————

———————————————————————————————

10. His desire for knowledge ————————————————————

———————————————————————————————

———————————————————————————————

11. The change which Ernest underwent ——————————————

———————————————————————————————

———————————————————————————————

12. Ernest had fewer friends now, ————————————————

———————————————————————————————

———————————————————————————————

13. As his values changed, ————————————————————

———————————————————————————————

———————————————————————————————

B.   Answer each question with a complete sentence.

Example: How is your style?

My style is what I make of it.

1. Who has heard of Ernest? _____

2. What kind of a car did Ernest drive? _____

3. What kind of shoes did he wear? _____

4. What did Ernest pretend to know? _____

5. Who said that Ernest invented the expression "life style"? _____

6. Was it the truth that Ernest invented the expression "life style"? ____

7. What was the truth? _____

8. How was the language Ernest used? _____

9. What kind of words did he use? _____

10. Why was Ernest unable to think simply and directly? _____

11. What did Ernest try in vain? _____

12. Why did his friends stay with him? _____

13. What happened when Ernest became aware that his suspicions were true? _____

14. What caused Ernest to become poor? _____

15. How did Ernest change when he became poor? _____

16. What did he begin doing? _____

17. Where did Ernest spend his afternoons? _____

18. To whom did he become a familiar figure? _____

19. Why was his desire for knowledge endless? _____

20. What was the change that Ernest underwent? _____

21. What type of car did he drive now? _____

22. How were his friends now? _____

23. Why did his style change? _____

IX. Commentary on Model

A.   Write about the **lesson** you've learned from the MODEL COMPOSITION.

B.   Write about the points you agree with.

C.   Write about the points you disagree with.

D.   Give an appropriate title to your composition.

X. Composition

A.   Using the key words and phrases from the MODEL COMPOSITION, write your own composition on a related topic. Use the style of the MODEL COMPOSITION.

"show off"	pretend	spend	thrifty
"life style"	cheap	vulgar	orderly
fruitless	suspect	friends	amuse
control	habits	excessive	poor
library	read	knowledge	change
generous	simple	sincere	suspicions
recognize	economy	values	amuse

B.   Select one topic and express your ideas about it in any **form** of writing.

    1. Desire for knowledge comes to poor people.

2. The value of learning is great.

3. Ignorance is better than knowledge.

4. A tree is a beautiful thing of nature.

5. Nature is full of miracles.

C.   Describe the picture below in any **style** of writing you choose.

Appendix

I. The Principal Parts of Irregular Verbs

A complete list of **irregular** verbs and their principal parts can be found in every good dictionary. Included here for the convenience of the reader are some more commonly used irregular verbs and their principal parts.

The first principal part of a verb is the **infinitive** (simple form of the verb), the second principal part is the **past tense** and the third principal part is the **past participle**. We don't ordinarily consider the **present participle** to be one of the principal parts because it is always regular and is quite simple to construct; i.e., be = being, go = going, have = having, do = doing, etc.

Infinitive	Past Tense	Past Participle
awake	awaked, awoke	awaked
be	was, were	been
become	became	become
begin	began	begun
bleed	bled	bled
blow	blew	blown
break	broke	broken
bring	brought	brought
build	built	built
buy	bought	bought
catch	caught	caught
choose	chose	chosen
come	came	come
deal	dealt	dealt
dig	dug	dug
dive	dived, dove	dived
do	did	done
draw	drew	drawn
dream	dreamt, dreamed	dreamt, dreamed
drink	drank	drunk
drive	drove	driven
eat	ate	ate
fall	fell	fallen
feel	felt	felt
fight	fought	fought
find	found	found
fly	flew	flown
forget	forgot	forgot, forgotten
forgive	forgave	forgiven
get	got	got, gotten
give	gave	given
go	went	gone

grow	grew	grown
hang	hung, hanged	hung, hanged
have	had	had
hear	heard	heard
hide	hid	hidden
hold	held	held
keep	kept	kept
know	knew	known
lay	laid	laid
leave	left	left
lie (recline)	lay	lain
lie (tell a lie)	lied	lied
lose	lost	lost
make	made	made
meet	met	met
pay	paid	paid
read	read	read
run	ran	run
say	said	said
see	saw	seen
sell	sold	sold
send	sent	sent
shoot	shot	shot
sing	sang	sung
sit	sat	sat
sleep	slept	slept
speak	spoke	spoken
speed	sped	sped
spend	spent	spent
stand	stood	stood
steal	stole	stolen
swim	swam	swum
take	took	taken
teach	taught	taught
tell	told	told
think	thought	thought
throw	threw	thrown
understand	understood	understood
wake	waked, woke	woke
wear	wore	worn
win	won	won
wind	wound	wound
withdraw	withdrew	withdrawn
write	wrote	written

II. Parts of Speech

This brief glossary serves the purpose of a rapid review of the parts of speech in their most common usage. Most of the material described here has been discussed in detail within appropriate chapters of the book. Some definitions are followed by typical examples of usage.

A.   The NOUN is a word that names a **person, place, thing, quality, state of being** or **action**. The noun has **number, gender** and **case**. It is used in every complete sentence as a **subject**. There are concrete (physical) nouns and there are abstract (idea) nouns. Examples: concrete = table, book, bread; abstract = happiness, love, thought.

B.   The PRONOUN is a **substitute for a noun** or a noun equivalent. There are several kinds of pronouns:

1. The Personal Pronoun—I, you, he, she, we, etc.

2. The Demonstrative Pronoun—this, that, these, those

3. The Indefinite Pronoun—anybody, somebody, many, each, one, some, etc.

4. The Relative Pronoun—that, who, which, etc.

5. The Interrogative Pronoun—who?, which?, what?, etc.

6. The Reflexive Pronoun—myself, yourself, etc.

C.   The VERB usually tells something about the **action** of the subject. The verb may also express **condition** or **state of being**. There are four types of verbs:

1. The Transitive Verb—tells what the subject does to an object, a person, a thing or a place.

2. The Intransitive Verb—does not need an object to complete its meaning. The intransitive verb tells something about what the subject is.

3. The Linking Verb—is a special kind of intransitive verb. It functions as a connection between a **subject** and a **predicate complement**.

4. The Auxiliary Verb—helps other verbs to express **action** or **condition** or **state** of **being**.

D. The ADJECTIVE describes a noun or a pronoun. It is neither singular nor plural. The adjective can compare one noun to another. Adjectives are classified according to their function:

1. The Descriptive Adjective—**describes** the noun or the pronoun.

2. The Limiting Adjective—**limits** or **defines** the meaning of the noun or the pronoun.

E. The ARTICLE comes in two forms:

1. The Definite Article—the

2. The Indefinite Article—a, one, an

The is used with a singular or plural noun; **a** is commonly used with a singular noun.

F. The ADVERB modifies and changes in some way the meaning of a **verb**, an **adjective** or another **adverb**. The following are the most commonly used types of adverbs:

1. The Adverb of TIME—answers the question **when?**, i.e., **recently, soon, immediately, now, then, first, later, always, never, often**, etc.

2. The Adverb of PLACE—answers the question **where?**, i.e., **here, away, west, everywhere**, etc.

3. The Adverb of MANNER—answers the question **how?**, i.e., **quickly, slowly, badly, well**, etc.

G. A PREPOSITION shows the **relationship** between a **noun** or a **pronoun** and another word. The preposition generally expresses the relation of one thing to another in regard to:

1. **time**—i.e. **before** noon, **after** the holidays, **until** midnight, etc.

2. **manner**—i.e. **with** happiness, **by** mistake, etc.

3. **position** or **place**—i.e. **at** the airport, **at** home, **in** the house, **on top of** the mountain, etc.

H. A CONJUNCTION **connects** words or groups of words. There are two types of conjunctions:

     1. Coordinating—joins equal grammatical units, i.e. Mary **and** Kip **and** Susan **and** Joe, Don **or** Sheila, etc. I'll tell you **if and when** I get ready. He'll do it at nine A.M. **or** after ten.

     2. Subordinating—introduces a clause that depends on a **main** or independent clause; i.e.

       a. **time (as, before, when, while**, etc.)

       b. **reason** or **cause (because, since, why**, etc.)

       c. **supposition** or **condition (although, unless, whether. . . .or**, etc.)

I.   The INTERJECTION serves to express **emotion**. It is generally followed by an **exclamation mark** (!), i.e. OH! HELP! HURRAH! etc.

Index

A

B

C

D

E

F

G

Q

R

T

Tense, 41, 43, 47
   future, 177
   future perfect, 118
   logical sequence, 108, 118
   past, 117
   past perfect, 118
   past progressive, 117
   present, 117
   present perfect, 117
   present progressive, 117
Term paper, 203, 207
   bibliography card, 203
   note card, 203
   outline, 203
   title page, 203
Texas, 46
The War Years, 144
The Winds of War, 144
Time, 81, 91, 116
Transformation, 41, 46
Transitive (verb), 41

V

Verbs, 23, 40*ff.*, 46
   intransitive, 41
   irregular, 258-9
   linking, 41
   principal parts, of, 258-9
   tense, 116*ff.*
   transitive, 41
Virtue, 244
Vowel, 8

W